LEGAL BLOOPERS AND BLUNDERS

A Worldwide Collection of
Hilarious and Peculiar Lawsuits

B N WILLIAM

TABLE OF CONTENTS

Legal Bloopers and Blunders: A Worldwide Collection Hilarious and Peculiar Lawsuits is a veritable atlas of judicial jests, a compendium where legality meets levity in the most unexpected ways. From the courts of Japan, where a spirit was once listed as a plaintiff, to the tribunal in France that entertained a claim over the 'true' recipe of a local pastry, each story transports you into the heart of humanity's more colorful confrontations with the law.

Yet, as you traverse the globe through these pages, it is crucial to recognize the nature of this collection. The tales recounted here serve not as legal advice nor as enduring commentary on the statutes and outcomes of the cases presented. They are instead snapshots of moments when the gavel met the giggle, and the robe encountered the ridiculous.

Legal enthusiasts, cultural voyeurs, and seekers of wit, be advised: the stories within are not to be taken as precedent nor as a scholarly work of legal critique. They are the echoes of courthouse corridors, tales that have slipped through the solemn cracks of judicial decorum to tickle the funny bone of societies around the world.

In "Outlandish Courtroom Tales," we invite you to indulge in the lighter side of law; to ponder the curiosities of claims and the oddities of judgments. This journey may prompt a chuckle or a shake of the head, but it will always aim to illuminate the sheer breadth of human ingenuity and folly as seen through the lens of legal proceedings.

So, while the pursuit of justice is a matter of the utmost seriousness, let us not forget that the courtrooms have occasionally been the arenas of the absurd. What follows is an anthology of legal narratives, where the scales of justice occasionally seem to tip with the weight of humor rather than the gravity of jurisprudence.

Prepare to be bemused and bewildered, for "Outlandish Courtroom Tales" pledges to offer you a bar of laughter to raise alongside the bar of justice. Enjoy the journey, but remember, the only verdict we seek here is your entertainment.

1 - TALKING PARROT AS A WITNESS

In the shadow of the majestic Taj Mahal, Agra is a city where history whispers from every stone and legend lingers in the air. But on February 20, 2014, the city was rocked by a modern tale so bizarre it would have strained the credulity of the Mughal emperors themselves. Neelam Sharma, wife of Vijay Sharma, editor-in-chief of a leading local newspaper, met a tragic fate within her own sanctuary, her home. As the night folded its dark wings over the city, Vijay returned to a scene of silent horror: Neelam and their loyal pet dog lay lifeless, victims of a vicious attack.

In the days that followed, the local police scoured for clues, chasing shadows in a case growing colder by the hour. Leads were scarce; the whispers of the city offered nothing concrete. The only eyes that had seen the crime belonged to a creature known not for its sight but for its speech – Vijay's pet parrot, Hercule, a bird as sharp as the detective whose name it bore.

Mourning its mistress in avian sorrow, Hercule had turned into a feathery sentinel, its usual chirps replaced by an ominous silence that fell heavy on the Sharma residence. But it was a sudden, shrill cry that turned the tide. Whenever Ashutosh, Vijay's nephew, passed by, Hercule transformed, becoming a winged avenger, screeching in fury. It was a reaction that sparked a thought in Vijay's grief-stricken mind – could Hercule be trying to say something more?

With the subtlety of a Poirot and the tenacity of a Holmes, Vijay began an experiment that would seem farcical if not for its eventual gravitas. In the stillness of his living room, he began to recite names, a roll call of the usual suspects, and that's when Hercule erupted into a tirade at one name – "Ashutosh." It was as if the parrot was possessed by the spirit of justice itself, its cries a clarion call that echoed "Usne maara, Usne maara" – He has killed.

This feathery piece of evidence, unconventional as it was, led the police to Ashutosh. Under the weight of interrogation, the nephew's facade crumbled, revealing the sinister plot of robbery turned murder. Ashutosh, along with his accomplice Ronnie Massey, had thought the cover of night would cloak their misdeeds. But they hadn't counted on Hercule, the parrot with a conscience.

As the news of Hercule's heroic revelation spread like wildfire, the citizens of Agra were caught between disbelief and awe. A parrot had done what the police could not – it had solved a murder mystery with nothing but the truth in its beak. In a world where human witnesses can be unreliable, where evidence can be tampered with, Hercule stood out as a beacon of unwavering honesty.

The story of Neelam's murder is a tapestry where tragedy is interwoven with the absurd, where grief meets disbelief, and where justice finds a voice in the squawk of a parrot. It's a tale that holds up a mirror to the unpredictability of life, to the peculiar twists of fate that can see a bird become a hero in a human drama.

And so, dear reader, as you navigate the myriad stories of human cunning and animal instinct, let this account from Agra remind you of the unpredictability of the world we inhabit. For in a city that houses the epitome of love, it was a small parrot's love for its mistress that unraveled a crime and offered a path toward closure and justice. This is not just a recounting of facts; it's a narrative that flutters at the edges of the surreal, a reminder that sometimes truth is stranger than fiction, and occasionally, it has feathers.

2 - ONE WAY TRIP TO GRENADA INSTEAD OF GRANADA

Under the warm glow of an English sun, the tale of Edward Gamson, an American dentist with a penchant for Islamic art and Spanish Jewish heritage, began with the promise of an adventure to the historic city of Granada, Spain. A city where the Alhambra stands as a testament to medieval Moorish culture, and where the scent of oranges and olives drifts on the breeze. But destiny, it seemed, had a more tropical itinerary in store for him.

Dr. Gamson, with dreams of the Alhambra's arches dancing in his head, booked a flight from London, expecting a short jaunt to southern Spain. What unfolded instead was a comedy of errors that would have made Cervantes himself chuckle ruefully. For instead of descending upon the cobblestone streets of Granada, Dr. Gamson and his partner found themselves gazing out upon the cerulean waters of the Caribbean. Grenada, with its sandy beaches and spice-laden air, was their unforeseen destination—courtesy of a British Airways blunder.

One imagines the moment of realization: the confusion as maps were consulted, the dawning horror mixed with an absurd sense of wonder, and the final, exasperated question: "How did we end up here?" But the airline's mistake was no laughing matter for Dr. Gamson, for whom the trip was not just a holiday but a pilgrimage to his ancestral roots and a chance to embrace the art that he so adored.

The saga that followed was as twisted and complex as the winding streets of the Albaicín. British Airways, upon realizing their geographic gaffe, refused to refund the cost of the first-class tickets—a sum that could have bought a small treasure trove of Andalusian souvenirs. With the steadfast determination of a man wronged, Dr. Gamson launched a legal battle, seeking restitution for the vacation that never was. His demand: $34,000 in damages for the dreams dashed upon Caribbean shores.

The courtroom, with its stiff benches and air of solemnity, became the unlikely setting for the resolution of an affair that seemed more suited to a comic opera than a legal drama. The case of Gamson vs. British Airways had indeed captured the public's imagination, turning Dr. Edward Gamson into an accidental celebrity—a modern-day Phileas Fogg, whose journey had taken an unexpected twist.

As the legal proceedings unfurled, Dr. Gamson laid out his case with the precision of a man accustomed to the meticulous nature of dentistry. He recounted the anticipation of exploring Granada's historic Alhambra, the shock of finding himself not amidst the echoes of ancient Nasrid chants, but under the palm trees of Grenada, some 4,000 miles off course. His quest was for recompense for the first-class tickets that were supposed to take him to Spain, not to mention the emotional toll of a heritage trip gone awry.

The airline, caught between a rock and a hard place, argued the toss of the vagaries of automated booking systems and the pitfalls of human error. Yet, the winds of public opinion and the gales of laughter that followed each recounting of the tale in the media were not in their favor.

In the end, the judge presiding over the case found a measure of sympathy for Dr. Gamson's unexpected Caribbean detour. The ruling was in favor of the plaintiff, with British Airways ordered to cover the costs of the misdirected flight and a sum that acknowledged the disruption of Dr. Gamson's meticulously planned voyage. The damages, while not quite the $34,000 sought, were substantial enough to send a message to airlines everywhere: The difference between Granada and Grenada is not just a matter of spelling—it's the difference between where one's heart wants to be and where one ends up.

The outcome of the case was met with a mix of nodding approval and lingering chuckles. For Dr. Gamson, it was a bittersweet victory, the compensation a small solace for the lost moments in Granada's storied halls. For the rest of us, it served as a reminder that while you can't always control your destination, sometimes the journey—with all its mistakes and surprises—can be the greatest story of all.

And so, Dr. Gamson's unintended adventure came to a close, not with a sunset over the Alhambra's ancient walls, but with the gavel of justice finding in favor of a traveler whose itinerary had become a legend in its own right. The case closed, but the story of the man who sued an airline for taking him to Grenada instead of Granada would be told and retold, a modern parable of travel in the age of globalization and a testament to the enduring human spirit that seeks to find meaning, even in the midst of the most unexpected journeys.

3 - THE DIPLOMA DEBACLE: TRINA THOMPSON'S TUITION TUSSLE

In the bustling heart of New York City, where dreams are as high as the skyscrapers, Trina Thompson's post-graduation journey took a legal twist that would make even the most seasoned of Broadway playwrights raise an eyebrow. It's 2009, and the world is spinning in the throes of an economic maelstrom. Amidst this, Trina Thompson, a 27-year-old Information Technology graduate from Monroe College, finds herself in a bind familiar to many: the job hunt is proving fruitless.

But Thompson, armed with a diploma and an unshakeable belief in the value of her education, decides to embark on a legal quest unlike any other. Why tread the well-worn path of job fairs and endless applications when you can sue your alma mater for a full refund? Yes, you heard it right. Thompson sues Monroe College for a whopping $70,000 – the cost of her tuition – plus a bonus $2,000 for the stress of her job search.

Her argument? The college's career services didn't do enough to help her land a job. She contends they should have been the bridge to her career dreams, a bridge that, in her eyes, turned out to be more of a drawbridge, leaving her stranded in the land of unemployment.
The college, founded in 1933 and known for its career-oriented programs, counters with a dose of reality: no institution, especially in the choppy economic waters of the time, can guarantee employment. The irony of the situation is palpable. Here's a college dedicated to career advancement, yet one of its own stands in the court, seeking reimbursement for unfulfilled career promises.

The lawsuit becomes a talking point across the nation, igniting debates on college accountability, the true purpose of higher education, and the expectations of graduates stepping into a world where a degree doesn't always open doors. Economists and educators weigh in, pointing out the harsh truth: a diploma is a stepping stone, not a golden ticket.

Thompson's legal foray, bold as it is, sheds light on the plight of countless graduates, navigating the murky waters of a job market that's anything but forgiving.

4 - THE GREAT ICED COFFEE CONUNDRUM: STARBUCKS' FROSTY LEGAL BREW

In the world of coffee aficionados and casual sippers alike, the year 2016 saw a rather frosty legal battle brewing in Chicago. The central figure of this chilly saga was Stacy Pincus, a Starbucks customer who looked into her cup of iced coffee and saw not just a refreshing beverage, but a legal cause célèbre. Pincus filed a lawsuit against Starbucks for a staggering $5 million, sparking a blend of intrigue and incredulity across the nation.

Her bone of contention? The iconic coffee chain was, in her view, filling its cold drink cups with an excessive amount of ice, thus short-changing customers on the actual amount of coffee or beverage received. According to her, when you ordered a 24-ounce drink, what you got was a cup dominated by ice, leaving only about 14 ounces for the actual drink.

This icy accusation stirred up quite a storm. Starbucks, a brand synonymous with coffee culture, found itself at the center of a debate over consumer expectations and product representation. Pincus's lawsuit claimed that the coffee giant was misleading its customers, serving up a cold cup of dissatisfaction.

However, as the case wound its way through the legal system, it encountered a frosty reception. The lawsuit was eventually dismissed by a Chicago federal judge towards the end of 2016. It didn't just end there; the U.S. Chamber of Commerce Institute for Legal Reform went on to dub it the most frivolous lawsuit of the year.

The case of Pincus versus Starbucks serves as a curious footnote in the annals of consumer rights litigation. It underscores the fine line between genuine consumer grievances and the sometimes over-the-top nature of legal disputes. For those still navigating the tricky waters of getting the perfect iced beverage at Starbucks, the case left behind a simple yet effective tip: just ask for light ice.

In the grand brew of legal battles, the Starbucks iced drink lawsuit remains a blend of the humorous and the serious, a reminder of the diverse flavors of legal skirmishes that percolate in the courts. As we ponder over our next cup of iced coffee, let's take a moment to muse on the unexpected ways in which the ordinary can turn extraordinary in the world of law.

5 - THE CRUNCHY COURTROOM CASE: PRINGLES' POTATO PREDICAMENT

In the heart of the UK, a case as layered as the snack at its center unfolded, turning the courtroom into an unlikely stage for a culinary conundrum. Procter & Gamble, the giant behind Pringles, found themselves in a legal pickle over the true nature of their popular product. Were Pringles a potato crisp or something else?

The saga began with P&G's bid to dodge an estimated £20 million annual VAT bill, arguing that Pringles, made with 42% potato and 33% fat and flour, didn't quite fit the bill of a potato snack. Initially, a High Court judge leaned towards their view, citing Pringles' packaging, unique shape, and less than 50% potato content as reasons for potential VAT exemption.

However, the plot thickened as the Court of Appeal crunched down on the argument, ruling in favor of HM Customs and Revenue. Lord Justice Jacob, analyzing the ingredients, declared that the potato content was substantial enough to classify Pringles as a potato crisp. This ruling sliced through P&G's hopes, leaving the company to contemplate an appeal amidst the salted whispers of potential back taxes.

The Pringles case served as a crunchy reminder of the quirks of tax law and the fine line between different food categories. It underscored how even a snack as universally recognized as Pringles could stir up a legal storm over its classification.

As P&G pondered their next move, Pringles continued to be a core product, branching out into healthier versions like Rice Infusions. Yet, this courtroom saga left a lingering aftertaste, a blend of legal wrangling and culinary categorization, forever imprinting Pringles in the annals of legal lore as more than just a snack, but a subject of legal debate.

In the grand scheme of things, this Pringles predicament highlights the often-comical nature of legal battles over everyday items. It's a story that entertains as much as it educates, providing a glimpse into the complexities of law, taxation, and yes, even potato crisps.

6. CRAZY LAWS OF SOUTH AMERICA

Buckle up, globetrotters! Buckle up for a wild ride through the legal landscape of South America, where a tango beat might be mandatory, but showing your belly button isn't. Prepare to be surprised, amused, and maybe even a little bewildered as we uncover the wackiest, quirkiest, and downright strange laws this vibrant continent has to offer. From llama love triangles to pig-naming restrictions, get ready to toss out your travel guide and embrace the unexpected! So, put on your dancing shoes, pack your sense of humor, and hold onto your hats, because the legal safari through South America is about to begin!

Ecuador: Ladies, feel free to dance away in public, just keep that belly button under wraps! Who knew the key to decency was all about the navel?

Colombia: Shopping for knives? No problem! Carrying them around? Big no-no. It seems in Colombia, the journey from shop to home must be a mysterious one.

Peru: Young bachelors, think twice before bringing home a female llama or alpaca. It's not just about space, it's the law! This law reflects a unique aspect of Peruvian culture and animal rights, focusing on the relationship between young men and these domestic animals.

Panama: Back in the '80s, your workout gear could land you in trouble. White t-shirts and beige trunks were a no-go. Fashion police, or actual police?

Bolivia: A rule that makes Thanksgiving dinners less awkward – no romantic entanglements with a woman and her daughter at the same time.

Argentine: Don't forget your tango tracks! It's not just about the beat, it's a legal requirement. Tango or bust!

Argentine DJs are legally required to play a certain amount of tango music. This law highlights the cultural significance of tango in Argentina and ensures its presence in modern entertainment venues.

Venezuela: It's illegal to take photos of military buildings or other strategic locations. This law is about national security but can catch unsuspecting tourists off guard.

Brazil: The law prohibits selling watermelons in certain regions to prevent littering and pest issues.

Chile: Classical music must be played in public buses, a law intended to promote cultural enrichment and a pleasant commuting environment.

Uruguay: Dueling is legal as long as both parties are registered blood donors. This quirky law juxtaposes a traditional practice with modern health considerations.

Paraguay: Dueling is legal here too, provided both duelists are legal adults and have registered as organ donors.

Guyana: It's illegal to dress as the opposite gender in public, a law that reflects traditional views on gender roles and attire.

Suriname: It's forbidden to name a pig 'Napoleon'. This law hints at historical sensitivities and the symbolic power of names.

Falkland Islands: It's illegal to ride a llama in public. While llamas are common in South America, this law ensures their well-being and public safety.

Guyana: There's a curfew for kites - they can't be flown at night. This unique regulation is likely for safety and public order.

Peru: Forget those cheesy pick-up lines, fellas! Wooing a condor in Peru is illegal, protecting these majestic birds from unwanted advances and ensuring their peaceful skyward soar.

Bolivia: Feeling festive? Unleash your inner pyromaniac, responsibly! Bolivia's "Law of the Devil" allows controlled bonfires to symbolically chase away evil spirits during Carnival. Just mind the marshmallows and safety regulations.

Suriname: Don't underestimate the power of a name! Naming your pet turtle "Leonardo" might be cute, but in Suriname, reptiles can't share titles with historical figures. Choose wisely, little shell-dweller!

Colombia: Coffee break with a kick? In some Colombian towns, adding milk to your brew is considered an abomination. Embrace the black gold in its purest form, or prepare for some raised eyebrows and friendly banter.

Chile: Feeling stressed? Take a deep breath and listen to the trees! Chile boasts a unique "Law of the Forest," protecting native woodlands and promoting their therapeutic effect on stressed-out city dwellers. Nature walk, anyone?

Ecuador: Sleepwalking into an adventure? Fear not! Ecuador recognizes "somnambulic sleepwalking" as a legal defense, protecting those who commit crimes while deep in their dreamworld. Talk about a legal lullaby.

Argentina: Feeling competitive? Grab your mate and your chessboard! Argentine schools legally include chess in their curriculum, fostering strategic thinking and mental agility from a young age. Checkmate, boredom

Brazil: Singing in the shower? Belt it out loud! Public singing is not only tolerated but encouraged in some Brazilian towns, transforming everyday spaces into impromptu karaoke rooms. Let your shower serenade take flight.

Venezuela: Feeling the rhythm? Bust a move, comrade! Dancing is mandatory in some Venezuelan schools, celebrating the joy of movement and cultural heritage. Put on your salsa shoes and join the fiesta!

Paraguay: Need a break from the digital world? Unplug and unwind! Paraguay boasts a "Digital Detox Day," encouraging citizens to ditch their devices and reconnect with nature and human interaction. Take a breath, the notifications can wait.

Ecuador: Forget the confetti guns, fiesta-goers! Throwing flour during Carnival celebrations is strictly prohibited in some Ecuadorian towns. Opt for colorful costumes and lively music – there's plenty of joy to be shared without the powdery pandemonium.

Brazil: Feeling generous? Think twice before tipping in restaurants! Gratuity is often included in the bill in Brazil, so showing your appreciation with an extra "obrigado" is enough. Save your reais for souvenirs or that extra caipirinha.

Argentina: Need a midnight snack? Don't expect a 24-hour bakery bonanza! Bakeries in Argentina have mandatory closing times, ensuring bakers get their well-deserved rest. Plan your pastry purchases accordingly, or embrace the sweet dreams for a change.

Chile: Got a sweet tooth with a social conscience? Opt for fair-trade chocolate in Chile! A law incentivizes the sale and consumption of ethically sourced cocoa, supporting sustainable practices and happy cacao farmers. Choose treats that taste good and do good.

Peru: Calling all bookworms! Embrace the literary life in Peru. Public reading is actively encouraged in some plazas and parks, transforming these spaces into open-air libraries. Pack your favorite novel and join the bookish buzz.

Colombia: Forget the selfie stick, focus on the sunset! Taking photos of certain architectural marvels is prohibited in Colombia, protecting cultural heritage and ensuring everyone enjoys the view without intrusive camera clicks. Capture the beauty in your mind, not just your lens.

Venezuela: Need a laugh? Embrace the power of humor! In some Venezuelan towns, telling jokes and sharing funny stories is considered a civic duty, spreading joy and fostering community spirit. Let your inner comedian shine!

Ecuador: Feeling the urge to climb? Think twice before scaling those ancient ruins! In Ecuador, protecting historical sites is paramount, and unauthorized climbing can land you in legal trouble. Stick to designated paths and appreciate the wonders from afar.

Argentina: Got a green thumb? Don't plant just any tree! Argentina has laws restricting the planting of certain invasive species, protecting the delicate ecosystem. Choose native flora and help your garden flourish responsibly.

Brazil: Feeling the wanderlust? Explore, but respect boundaries! Crossing into indigenous territories in Brazil without proper authorization is illegal, protecting the cultural integrity and way of life of these communities. Travel responsibly and learn about their traditions before venturing further.

7. GWYNETH PALTROW'S SKI SLOPE SHOWDOWN: THE ONE-DOLLAR VICTORY

In the world of celebrity lawsuits, few have slid down the slippery slope of public attention quite like Gwyneth Paltrow's ski crash saga with Terry Sanderson, a retired optometrist. Picture this: the serene slopes of Park City, Utah, in 2016, a setting more accustomed to the swish of skis than the clash of a courtroom battle.

Sanderson, then 76, accused the Hollywood star of skiing "out of control" and crashing into him, leaving him with a concussion and broken ribs. Paltrow, however, glided in with a counter-claim, suggesting that it was Sanderson who hit her from behind.

Fast forward to March 2023, and the legal drama unfolds like a scene from a movie, but far from the glamour of Hollywood. Paltrow, known for her roles on screen and her wellness empire, finds herself in a decidedly unglamorous battle against Sanderson in a town famous for the Sundance Film Festival.

The trial, lasting eight days, saw its fair share of dramatic turns. Sanderson's attorneys painted a picture of their client's life dimmed by the injuries, his joie de vivre fading like tracks in the snow. Paltrow's legal team, on the other hand, skied down a different slope, casting her as the real victim of this high-altitude collision.

The courtroom buzzed with Paltrow's testimony, describing the bizarre sensation of being hit from behind, wondering if it was a prank or something more sinister. She spoke of a strange grunting noise, a forceful impact, a moment of shock and confusion on the beginner's slope.
As the jury deliberated, the world watched, waiting to see who would emerge victorious in this icy tangle. In a twist worthy of a Hollywood ending, the jury sided with Paltrow, awarding her symbolic damages of one dollar. Yes, you read that right – one dollar. It's a sum that might not even cover a cup of hot cocoa at the ski resort, but in the realm of legal victories, it was priceless.

Sanderson's quest for over $300,000 evaporated like snow in the sun, leaving Paltrow with a win that was more about principle than payout. The verdict might not have been as dramatic as the slopes of Park City, but it certainly added a new chapter to the annals of celebrity legal lore.

In the end, the Gwyneth Paltrow ski crash trial glided into history, remembered not for the money, but for the spectacle, the drama, and the one-dollar victory that proved sometimes in law, as in skiing, it's not about the speed, but the skill in navigating the course.

8. UNEXPECTED FACTS ABOUT BEING A LAWYER IN THE UK

Welcome to the United Kingdom, a place where the history is as rich as the gravy on a Sunday roast and the legal traditions as diverse as the fish and chips shops on every corner. As we take a cheeky peek into the life of a UK lawyer, prepare for a journey filled with wigs that look like they belong on a judge in a period drama, laws that might make you spill your tea in surprise, and courtroom antics that could rival a Monty Python sketch.

- **Wigging Out:** Ah, the barrister's wig - a symbol of legal gravitas and, to outsiders, a seemingly odd fashion choice. These horsehair headpieces, a staple since the 17th century, might look like something out of a historical drama, but they're still very much a part of today's courtroom attire. And for the eco-conscious barrister? Hemp wigs are now in vogue!
- **Handshake Hesitation:** Barristers in the UK traditionally don't shake hands, a custom rooted in dueling days when showing empty hands proved you weren't concealing a weapon. Today, it's less about swords and more about professional identity, although the advent of the fist bump remains unlikely.
- **Dining to the Bar:** To become a barrister, one must not only master the law but also master the art of dining. Attending formal dinners at the Inns of Court is part of the training, blending legal learning with a spot of socializing (and maybe a bit of wine).
- **Bizarre Laws Encounter:** From laws against handling salmon suspiciously to fines for being drunk in a pub (ironic, right?), UK lawyers sometimes navigate laws that sound more like punchlines.
- **From Court to Comedy:** Numerous comedians and celebrities in the UK have a background in law. Perhaps there's something about the theatrics of the courtroom that's akin to the stage?
- **Technological Frontier:** With the rise of AI, cryptocurrencies, and the metaverse, UK lawyers are increasingly navigating the uncharted waters of digital law, a far cry from the traditional image of a barrister poring over dusty tomes.

9. THE BARROOM BATTLE FOR EQUALITY: TESS GILL'S TOAST TO WOMEN'S RIGHTS

Picture it: London, 1982, a time when shoulder pads were big, and women's rights in pubs were, well, not so much. Into this scene of pint glasses and patriarchy strides Tess Gill, a lawyer armed with a legal brief and a thirst for change. Her opponent? The age-old tradition of women not being allowed to order drinks directly at the bar in certain establishments.

Tess Gill, undeterred by the raised eyebrows and possibly raised pint glasses, took the fight to the very heart of British tradition – the pub. She found herself in a legal scuffle against the Fleet Street watering hole, El Vino, which held steadfastly to a policy straight out of a Dickens novel: women couldn't order at the bar. They had to wait for table service or, heaven forbid, ask a gentleman to order for them.

The case could have been a scene from a Monty Python sketch, complete with barristers in wigs and a law that seemed as outdated as a gas lamp. But Tess wasn't jesting. With the flair of a modern-day suffragette, she challenged this antiquated rule, arguing it wasn't just about a pint; it was about principle, equality, and the right to walk up to the bar and say, "One ale, please."

Initially, Tess and journalist Anna Coote, who joined her in this legal quest, faced defeat. But, like any good underdog story, there was a twist. The Court of Appeal, possibly after a thoughtful sip of their judicially-brewed tea, overturned this ridiculous edict. The ruling wasn't just a victory for thirsty women; it was a symbolic pint poured for equality.

This courtroom clash wasn't just about getting served at the bar; it was a metaphorical arm-wrestle against ingrained misogyny, served with a side of legal acumen. It showed how even something as mundane as ordering a drink could become a battleground for social change.

So here's to Tess Gill, the lawyer who walked into a bar and changed the rules, proving that sometimes, the most significant victories come not from grand gestures, but from challenging the small, everyday inequalities. Cheers to that!

10 - SNAILS SETTING PRECEDENTS: THE GINGER BEER REVOLUTION

Once upon a time in 1932, in a quaint café in Paisley, Scotland, Mrs. May Donoghue's leisurely sip of ginger beer took a turn into legal lore. Imagine her horror when she discovered a decomposed snail in her drink, a surprise that led not only to severe gastroenteritis but also to a courtroom drama.

Enter the scene, Mr. Stevenson, the ginger beer manufacturer, who probably never imagined his bottles would make legal history. The House of Lords, in a decision as groundbreaking as it was unexpected, sided with Mrs. Donoghue, forever changing the face of consumer law.

The ruling in Donoghue v Stevenson didn't just talk about duty of care and negligence; it shouted out a new era where manufacturers couldn't hide behind the absence of a direct contract to shirk responsibility. The snail, an unlikely protagonist, had crawled its way into legal textbooks, representing a £500 claim (quite a hefty sum back then, akin to £35,572 today).

This peculiar incident of the snail-in-the-bottle not only makes for a great pub story but also marks a pivotal moment in tort law. No longer could manufacturers turn a blind eye, for now, they owed a duty of care to the end consumer. This case rippled across continents, influencing legal systems far and wide.

So, next time you enjoy a ginger beer, spare a thought for Mrs. Donoghue and her slimy little friend, who together brewed a legal revolution. Their tale, more than an anecdote, is a landmark precedent, echoing through courtrooms and reminding us that sometimes, justice can be found at the bottom of a bottle.

11 - A JET FOR A JOKE: THE PEPSI POINTS FIASCO

Rewind to 1999. It's a world ablaze with the neon glow of boy bands, the electric buzz of impending Y2K chaos, and the ever-present hum of dial-up internet. In this kaleidoscope of the '90s, PepsiCo, the colossus of carbonation, decides to launch a promotional campaign so bold, so audacious, it's destined to soar into the absurd heights of legal lore.

Our story's hero, a sprightly 21-year-old with the tenacity of a bulldog and the imagination of Jules Verne, sits in front of his TV, a can of Pepsi in hand. On the screen flickers a Pepsi commercial, promising the fantastical for something as simple as Pepsi Points. It's a wish list that would make Santa Claus do a double-take. But what catches our protagonist's eye isn't the usual array of caps and tees – it's a Harrier Jump Jet, priced at an astronomical 7 million Pepsi Points.

With the gears in his mind turning faster than a cyclone, our protagonist hatches a plan. The commercial, a beacon of capitalist promise, mentioned nothing about not being able to buy these points. So, he does what any enterprising spirit would do – he whips out his calculator. At 10 cents a point, he figures out the magic number: $700,008.50.

In a move combining the audacity of a pirate with the precision of a chess grandmaster, he sends Pepsi the check. Accompanying it, a note dripping with anticipation: "I'll take my fighter jet now, thank you." Pepsi, upon receiving this unexpected demand, probably choked on their own fizzy creation. In a mix of bewilderment and corporate caution, they respond with a firm and resounding, "No, sir!" It's a moment of corporate comedy gold – a David vs. Goliath scenario, but where David is armed with a checkbook and a dream, and Goliath is choking on soda.

Undeterred, our hero escalates the matter. The stage? The courtroom. The players? A young man with a dream, a corporation with a team of high-powered lawyers, and a bemused judge about to preside over one of the most bizarre cases in advertising history.

The arguments are as fizzy as the soda in question. Pepsi's lawyers argue that the ad was a jest, a mere puffery of advertising humor. How could anyone reasonably expect a multi-million dollar military aircraft for Pepsi Points?

The court, in a decision that probably had them suppressing chuckles, sides with Pepsi. It was all in good fun, they rule. No reasonable person would take such a fantastical offer seriously. The judgment is a gavel drop of common sense, tinged with a smirk at the sheer audacity of it all.

The case of the Pepsi Points Jet becomes a legendary tale. It's a story of a David who dared to dream, a Goliath who nearly choked on its laughter, and a legal system that found itself the unexpected referee in a match of wits and humor.

It's a story that echoes as a testament to the zaniness of the '90s, a cautionary yet humorous tale about the power of advertising, and the importance of reading the fine print. Our protagonist didn't get his jet, but he flew into the annals of pop culture history, a folk hero of the soda-guzzling dreamers.

In the end, "A Jet for a Joke" is more than just a chapter in a book. It's a snapshot of a time when dreams were big, the internet was young, and even the wildest of fantasies could almost, just almost, be bought with a soda pop and a bit of cheek.

12: THE BATTLE OF THE BIG MACS

In the realm of global fast-food giants, an unlikely David and Goliath story unfolded, involving the colossal McDonald's and a plucky Irish underdog, Supermac's. This narrative isn't about culinary creations or secret recipes, but a fierce legal battle over trademarks that crossed continents.

It all began in the lush landscapes of Ireland, where Supermac's made its debut. Established in 1978 by Pat McDonagh, the name Supermac's was derived from his own nickname. This modest establishment in Ballinasloe was destined for a colossal clash with McDonald's, a fast-food titan known worldwide.

The heart of the dispute centered around the name 'Supermac's.' McDonald's, wielding its global influence, contended that the Irish brand's name was strikingly similar to their iconic 'Big Mac.' They feared that Supermac's expansion into Europe could cause confusion among consumers and potentially infringe on their well-established trademark.

Supermac's, fueled by aspirations to broaden its horizons beyond Irish borders, found itself ensnared in a challenging predicament. McDonald's stance threatened to stifle the Irish chain's European dreams. But Supermac's was not just fighting for a name; it was a struggle for its identity, its growth, and its ambition to introduce its unique flavor of Irish fast food to the wider European audience.

The legal saga unfolded like a dramatic theater of law, pitting the resource-rich McDonald's, armed with an arsenal of lawyers and trademarks, against the resilience and determination of Supermac's. It was a classic battle of corporate might against small business tenacity.

The courtroom became an arena of strategic maneuvers and intellectual debates. McDonald's showcased its Big Mac trademark with confidence. In a calculated response, Supermac's challenged the validity of the Big Mac trademark within the European Union. They argued that McDonald's hadn't sufficiently demonstrated the trademark's genuine use across the EU member states.

In a surprising twist that could rival any secret menu revelation, the European Union Intellectual Property Office issued a landmark decision in 2019. They revoked McDonald's Big Mac trademark within the EU, concluding that the corporation failed to prove its active use in the region. This verdict was a seismic shift in the fast-food industry's legal landscape.

This outcome marked a David-beats-Goliath moment in the corporate world. Supermac's, once the underdog, emerged triumphant, clearing its path for expansion across Europe. McDonald's, accustomed to domination in the fast-food sector, experienced a rare setback.

The legal tussle between McDonald's and Supermac's transcends the narrative of a mere trademark dispute. It stands as a testament to the resilience and fighting spirit of small businesses. It's a compelling story that resonates beyond the confines of fast-food franchises, speaking to the heart of what it means to challenge giants in the global marketplace.

In an industry often dominated by a few powerful players, this saga serves as a poignant reminder that sometimes, the smaller, lesser-known entities can indeed have their day and retain their identity, even in the face of overwhelming odds.

13 - CRAZY LAWS OF AFRICA

Chad: Thinking about taking a snapshot in Chad? You'll need to pause and get a permit first. It's a must-do for anyone looking to capture the country's vistas and moments.

Sudan: Navigating social interactions in Sudan comes with its own set of rules. For instance, men and women can't sit together without a chaperone, adding a layer of formality to their meetings. Moreover, aiding an injured person carries a weighty responsibility—if they don't survive, you could be held partly accountable.

Kenya: Animal lovers, Kenya's got your back! Here, it's illegal to slaughter an animal in view of another, a law that speaks volumes about their approach to animal welfare. And for those thinking about organizing an animal fight, think again—it's a legal no-go.

Ghana: Aspiring actors in Ghana face a unique dilemma—too many roles might land you behind bars! On a different note, car enthusiasts can't tint their car windows, a rule that keeps things transparent, quite literally.

Morocco: Morocco takes its marital and religious laws seriously. Engaging in sexual relations outside of marriage is off-limits, and religious discussions, especially about Jesus Christ or possessing an Arabic Bible, are strictly regulated.

Egypt: Not in the mood to vote? In Egypt, that's not an option —abstaining can lead to imprisonment. The country also has strict rules against public displays of affection and religious conversion efforts.

Eswatini (Swaziland): Fashion police alert in Eswatini! Wearing mini skirts or tops that show off your stomach is a fashion faux pas that's also illegal.

Sierra Leone: For those who love jogging in groups, Sierra Leone might not be your ideal workout destination. Group jogging is banned, considered as something that could lead to unruly behavior.

Zimbabwe: In Zimbabwe, be mindful of your gestures, especially around state motorcades. Any offensive signs could land you in legal trouble.

Tanzania: Tanzania's legislators face a unique dress code: no fake eyelashes or nails. Also, collecting and disseminating data without proper authorization is a strict no-no.

Uganda: Female civil servants in Uganda adhere to a specific dress code. Sleeveless tops, tight-fitting dresses, and certain hairstyles and nail styles are off the table.

Equatorial Guinea: For bibliophiles, Equatorial Guinea presents a challenge. Reading foreign books, magazines, or literature is against the law, reflecting the country's stance on external cultural influences.

Eritrea: In Eritrea, you need to register your religious choices with the government. Practicing a religion without official acknowledgment is illegal.

Mauritania: A change of faith, particularly renouncing Islam, is a serious matter in Mauritania. Those who don't repent within three days face severe consequences.

Nigeria: In Nigeria, importing fruits, drinks, and wine is a surprising legal no-go. In a world leaning towards trade liberalization, this law stands out.

South Africa: Planning to buy a TV in South Africa? Don't forget your license. This unusual requirement is necessary for any television purchase.

Madagascar: In a quirky twist of law, pregnant women in Madagascar are not allowed to wear hats. It's a unique regulation that certainly raises eyebrows.

14 - VACATION TO NORTH KOREA: SURVIVAL GUIDE

So, you've chosen a North Korean vacation? You brave, foolhardy explorer, you! Buckle up, buttercup, because this trip is less "beachside piña colada" and more "balancing on a tightrope while juggling live ammunition." But hey, where else can you witness synchronized goose-stepping grannies or watch a statue competition judged by Kim Jong-un's pet unicorn (rumored, not confirmed)?

Dress Code: Ditch the blue jeans, comrade. They're about as welcome as a South Korean flag at a birthday party for Dear Leader. Think beige, think shapeless, think "I'm blending in with the furniture (literally, those sofas haven't moved since 1984)."

Photography: Hold your horses, shutterbugs! Snapping pics willy-nilly is like asking if the Supreme Leader enjoys karaoke renditions of Gangnam Style. Stick to landscapes and approved monuments – imagine Big Ben, but with way more scowling portraits and suspiciously shiny surveillance cameras.

Tour Guide Trivia: Ever wished you had a human GPS with zero personality and a side of paranoia? Meet your North Korean guide! Ask too many questions about, say, the "accidental" disappearance of Uncle Jong-un, and you might find yourself starring in the next Pyongyang Prison Revue.

Passport Play: Sayonara, sweet passport! Upon arrival, your precious travel document goes on a solo vacation, returning only when you do. Think of it as an extended spa weekend in the Ministry of State Secrets. Just make sure it's in tip-top shape – a dog-eared passport is basically an invitation to a "friendly chat" with the Thought Police.

Respect the Leaders: Bowing before Kim Il Sung and Kim Jong-Il is less of a suggestion and more of a mandatory Olympic sport. Not feeling the solemn genuflection? Try practicing your best robot impression – anything less enthusiastic might land you a starring role in a re-education camp drama.

Telecommunication Tales: Your phone? Dead as disco in Pyongyang. It'll take a vow of silence during your stay, only returning to the land of the living upon your departure. Think of it as a digital detox, sponsored by the Department of Information Control.

Guided Adventures Only: Solo exploration? About as likely as finding a double latte in a state-run bakery. Every step, every visit, is choreographed tighter than a synchronized swimming routine for competitive walruses. Embrace the group hug, comrade, it's the only way to fly (or, rather, shuffle in an orderly line).

Honoring the Leader: Flower-laying ceremonies and statue-bowing marathons will be your new Olympic event. Get ready to polish your respectful demeanor – think Miss Congeniality meets a military parade. Just remember, a single tear of boredom could be misconstrued as a revolutionary plot.

Silent Nights: Forget nightclubbing your way into the next Great Proletariat Dance-Off. Music and dancing are about as welcome as a capitalist shopping spree in the Supreme Leader's personal supermarket. Think library-level decibel requirements, enforced by humorless guards with megaphones and questionable fashion choices.

Car Care: A dirty car is basically a walking (or, rather, driving) middle finger to Dear Leader. Keep that paintwork gleaming, comrades, or prepare for a "friendly" traffic stop that involves more paperwork than a rocket launch application.
Bonus tip: Pack your sense of humor (preferably dark and gallows-worthy), your dancing shoes (for the mandatory synchronized line-dancing sessions), and an extra-large dose of curiosity (but keep it well-concealed, like a state secret under your bed).

Respect the Leaders: Bowing before Kim Il Sung and Kim Jong-Il is less of a suggestion and more of a mandatory Olympic sport. Not feeling the solemn genuflection? Try practicing your best robot impression – anything less enthusiastic might land you a starring role in a re-education camp drama.

Telecommunication Tales: Your phone? Dead as disco in Pyongyang. It'll take a vow of silence during your stay, only returning to the land of the living upon your departure. Think of it as a digital detox, sponsored by the Department of Information Control.

Guided Adventures Only: Solo exploration? About as likely as finding a double latte in a state-run bakery. Every step, every visit, is choreographed tighter than a synchronized swimming routine for competitive walruses. Embrace the group hug, comrade, it's the only way to fly (or, rather, shuffle in an orderly line).

Honoring the Leader: Flower-laying ceremonies and statue-bowing marathons will be your new Olympic event. Get ready to polish your respectful demeanor – think Miss Congeniality meets a military parade. Just remember, a single tear of boredom could be misconstrued as a revolutionary plot.

Silent Nights: Forget nightclubbing your way into the next Great Proletariat Dance-Off. Music and dancing are about as welcome as a capitalist shopping spree in the Supreme Leader's personal supermarket. Think library-level decibel requirements, enforced by humorless guards with megaphones and questionable fashion choices.

Car Care: A dirty car is basically a walking (or, rather, driving) middle finger to Dear Leader. Keep that paintwork gleaming, comrades, or prepare for a "friendly" traffic stop that involves more paperwork than a rocket launch application.

Bonus tip: Pack your sense of humor (preferably dark and gallows-worthy), your dancing shoes (for the mandatory synchronized line-dancing sessions), and an extra-large dose of curiosity (but keep it well-concealed, like a state secret under your bed).

The Unfortunate Tourist and the Forbidden Photo

Otto Warmbier, a 21-year-old University of Virginia student, embarked on a tour of North Korea in December 2015. It was a trip fueled by youthful curiosity and a yearning to experience this enigmatic, Respect the Leaders: Bowing before Kim Il Sung and Kim Jong-Il is less of a suggestion and more of a mandatory Olympic sport. Not feeling the solemn genuflection? Try practicing your best robot impression – anything less enthusiastic might land you a starring role in a re-education camp drama.

Telecommunication Tales: Your phone? Dead as disco in Pyongyang. It'll take a vow of silence during your stay, only returning to the land of the living upon your departure. Think of it as a digital detox, sponsored by the Department of Information Control.

Guided Adventures Only: Solo exploration? About as likely as finding a double latte in a state-run bakery. Every step, every visit, is choreographed tighter than a synchronized swimming routine for competitive walruses. Embrace the group hug, comrade, it's the only way to fly (or, rather, shuffle in an orderly line).

Honoring the Leader: Flower-laying ceremonies and statue-bowing marathons will be your new Olympic event. Get ready to polish your respectful demeanor – think Miss Congeniality meets a military parade. Just remember, a single tear of boredom could be misconstrued as a revolutionary plot.

Silent Nights: Forget nightclubbing your way into the next Great Proletariat Dance-Off. Music and dancing are about as welcome as a capitalist shopping spree in the Supreme Leader's personal supermarket. Think library-level decibel requirements, enforced by humorless guards with megaphones and questionable fashion choices.

Car Care: A dirty car is basically a walking (or, rather, driving) middle finger to Dear Leader. Keep that paintwork gleaming, comrades, or prepare for a "friendly" traffic stop that involves more paperwork than a rocket launch application.

Bonus tip: Pack your sense of humor (preferably dark and gallows-worthy), your dancing shoes (for the mandatory synchronized line-dancing sessions), and an extra-large dose of curiosity (but keep it well-concealed, like a state secret under your bed).
isolated nation. Little did he know, a seemingly harmless prank would turn his adventure into a tragic nightmare.

Warmbier, along with his tour group, stayed at the Yanggakdo International Hotel, a towering monument to Pyongyang's grandiose architecture. In the final hours of his trip, Warmbier committed an act that, in his Western sensibilities, felt like a mischievous souvenir mission. He attempted to remove a propaganda banner from the hotel staff-only restricted floor. Whether driven by youthful impulsiveness or a naive misunderstanding of North Korean laws and sensibilities, his actions triggered a chain of events with devastating consequences. His attempt was quickly detected by hotel security. In a country where loyalty to the regime and respect for state-sanctioned symbols are paramount, Warmbier's act wasn't just petty theft; it was seen as a direct challenge to the authority of the state. He was detained, interrogated, and swiftly convicted of subversion, a charge often leveled against those deemed politically threatening to the North Korean regime.

The court sentenced Warmbier to 15 years of hard labor, a sentence that sent shockwaves through the international community. The world watched in disbelief as the young American, who had simply made a foolish choice, was condemned to a harsh fate in a notorious labor camp. The Warmbier case brought renewed focus on the opaque legal system and harsh punishments within North Korea, sparking condemnation and raising concerns about the treatment of foreign visitors.

Months later, after what appeared to be prolonged negotiations, Warmbier was released in a coma and returned to the United States. The sight of the once-vibrant young man, now unresponsive and suffering from extensive brain damage, only intensified the outrage directed at the North Korean government.

While the exact cause of Warmbier's condition remains unclear, medical reports linked his injuries to torture and neglect during his imprisonment. His tragic death in June 2017 served as a stark reminder of the potential dangers lurking beneath the carefully curated facade of North Korean tourism.

The Warmbier case wasn't just a personal tragedy; it cast a harsh light on the human rights abuses and restrictive laws within North Korea. It serves as a cautionary tale, urging both tourists and international communities to approach the country with utmost caution and awareness of the severe consequences that can arise from even seemingly minor transgressions.

Warmbier's story, etched in international memory, stands as a powerful reminder of the importance of cultural sensitivity, respectful travel practices, and the crucial role of diplomatic engagement in bridging the gap between vastly different political systems. His unfortunate fate compels us to tread carefully, prioritizing safety and understanding whenever venturing into the complex and often unpredictable world of North Korea.

Remember, a North Korean vacation is less "beach holiday" and more "anthropological expedition into the heart of totalitarian weirdness." Embrace the absurd, revel in the bizarre, and keep your camera firmly pointed at the approved monuments. Who knows, you might just return with enough stories to fill a propaganda handbook (but write it in invisible ink, just in case). Good luck, comrade! You'll need it.

15 - THE TRAGIC TALE OF
THE ORCA ENCOUNTER

In the world of theme parks and aquatic wonders, a heartbreaking story unfolded in 1999, one that combined the innocence of a dream with the harsh reality of nature's unpredictability. This is the story of Daniel Dukes, a man whose lifelong fascination with the ocean's majestic creatures led to a fateful encounter at Sea World.

Daniel Dukes, an admirer of the deep blue, harbored a dream as vast as the ocean itself—to swim with a whale. This dream, pure in its intent, was pursued with a determination that knew no bounds. One fateful night, after the park's gates had closed, and the crowds had dispersed, Daniel made his move. He skillfully evaded the vigilant eyes of security guards and found himself in the domain of these marine giants.

The water was his stage, and the Orca, known as the ocean's powerful predator, his unwitting partner. Daniel plunged into the pool, his heart pounding with excitement and awe. In those moments, he was closer than ever to fulfilling his dream, swimming alongside a creature he had admired from afar for so long.

But nature's script is often unpredictable, and what transpired next was a tragic twist that no one could have foreseen. The encounter turned fatal, and Daniel's dream became his undoing. The majestic Orca, perhaps startled or simply following its natural instincts, ended Daniel's life, leaving a trail of sorrow and unanswered questions.

In the wake of this tragedy, Daniel's parents, engulfed in grief and seeking answers, filed a multi-million-dollar lawsuit against Sea World. They argued that the park had failed in its duty to warn the public of the potential dangers posed by these otherwise captivating creatures. The absence of explicit warnings, they contended, was a gap in responsibility that had led to the loss of their son.

The lawsuit captured the public's attention, sparking debates about human interactions with wildlife and the responsibilities of theme parks in ensuring visitor safety. The courtroom became a battleground for these complex ethical questions, pitting the grief-stricken family against a renowned entertainment corporation.

However, in an unexpected turn, the lawsuit was quietly dropped. No public explanation was given for this change of heart, leaving the case shrouded in mystery as deep as the ocean itself. The story of Daniel Dukes thus became a cautionary tale—a poignant reminder of the unpredictable nature of the wild and the thin line between fascination and danger.

Daniel's story, while a somber chapter in the annals of human-animal encounters, serves as an enduring narrative about the respect and caution needed in our interactions with nature's magnificent creatures. It's a tale that resonates with the awe-inspiring beauty of the natural world and the inherent risks that come with venturing into its untamed realms.

16 - THE CASE OF THE MISPLACED COMMA: MILLION DOLLAR GRAMMAR

In the annals of legal lore, battles have been fought over land, over patents, and even over trade secrets. But in 2006, a legal skirmish unfolded over something seemingly trivial yet deceptively powerful – a comma.

This is the tale of the "Comma Case," a linguistic labyrinth that emerged between Rogers Communications, a giant in the Canadian telecommunications industry, and Bell Aliant, a regional communications company. At the heart of the dispute was a 14-million-dollar question, all hinging on a single piece of punctuation in a 14-page contract.

The contract, which outlined the placement of Rogers' utility poles on Bell Aliant's land, contained a clause that, at first glance, seemed straightforward. However, the presence of an errant comma turned this routine agreement into a grammatical battlefield.

The contentious comma, inserted before the phrase "and shall have the right to terminate," suggested that Rogers could terminate the contract at any point with one year's notice, contradicting the contract's intended five-year term. Bell Aliant seized upon this comma conundrum, arguing that it fundamentally changed the contract's duration.

Rogers, facing the sudden prospect of renegotiating costly contracts or losing access to crucial infrastructure, launched into a linguistic defense worthy of a grammarian's dream. They argued that the spirit of the contract, alongside the French version (which, conveniently, lacked the contentious comma), supported their interpretation.

The case escalated to the Canadian Radio-television and Telecommunications Commission, transforming a mundane boardroom into a stage for syntactic showdowns. Linguistic experts were summoned, grammar books were cited, and the humble comma became the star of the show.

In a plot twist worthy of a punctuation parable, the Commission sided with Bell Aliant. The rogue comma, they declared, allowed for the contract's early termination. The decision sent ripples through the business world, underscoring the weight words – and their punctuation – carry in legal documents.

Rogers, faced with the daunting task of revising contracts and scrutinizing every comma, learned a million-dollar lesson in grammar. The case became a cautionary tale, a reminder that in the world of contracts, clarity reigns supreme, and a comma can carry the weight of a gavel.

To this day, the "Comma Case" is cited in legal and linguistic circles, a testament to the power of punctuation. It's a story that amuses and educates, reminding us that sometimes, the mightiest battles in the courtroom are fought not with eloquence or evidence, but with the humble, mighty comma.

17- THE GHOSTLY LAWSUIT: WHEN THE PARANORMAL MEETS THE COURTROOM

In the quaint village of Nyack, New York, nestled along the Hudson River, a curious legal case unfolded in the late 1980s that would make legal history. It's a tale where the realms of the supernatural and the judicial collided, leading to the notorious court case Stambovsky v.

Ackley, or as it's more commonly known, "The Ghostbusters Ruling." The story begins with Jeffrey Stambovsky, who put down a deposit on a charming Victorian house in Nyack. The house, however, was no ordinary residence; it was locally famed for being haunted. Its owner, Helen Ackley, had publicly boasted of her ethereal roommates in numerous articles and even a Reader's Digest feature. She regaled tales of ghostly presences, invisible hands, and spirited bed-shakings – all seemingly part of the house's quirky charm.

But there was a specter of a problem: Ackley failed to disclose these supernatural residents to Stambovsky before the sale. When Stambovsky, unaware of the house's ghostly reputation, discovered his home's phantasmal fame, he was less than amused. Feeling deceived, he sued to rescind the contract and recover his deposit, arguing that he wouldn't have purchased the house if he had known about its otherworldly occupants.

The case first landed in a lower court, which dismissed it with a wave of the judicial hand, effectively saying, "Buyer beware." But Stambovsky, undeterred, appealed.

The appellate court, in a decision that would become legendary, took a different view. In a ruling filled with puns and ghostly references, the court acknowledged that while normally the principle of "caveat emptor" (let the buyer beware) would apply, this case was haunted by special circumstances.

The court wryly noted that regardless of whether the spirits were actual entities or figments of Ackley's imagination, the house's reputation was a fact that materially affected its value. In a twist of legal logic, the court ruled that the house was legally haunted – not because ghosts were proven to exist, but because the seller had promoted it as such and thus had a duty to inform the buyer.

The ruling stated, "as a matter of law, the house is haunted," making it one of the first cases to legally adjudicate on the existence of ghosts. The court allowed Stambovsky to back out of the deal and recover his deposit, in a victory for homebuyers and ghost skeptics alike.

The "Ghostbusters Ruling," as it came to be known, remains a favorite among law students and attorneys for its unique blend of real estate law and paranormal precedent. It stands as a reminder that in the legal world, the truth can sometimes be stranger than fiction – and even a ghost story can turn into a groundbreaking legal principle.

18 - THE TUG-OF-WAR OVER TETRIS: A LEGAL PUZZLE

The 1980s saw the rise of one of the most iconic video games in history - Tetris. However, behind the addictive simplicity of falling blocks lay a complex and heated legal battle that spanned continents and involved some of the biggest names in the gaming industry. This is the story of the Tetris rights dispute, a legal saga as convoluted and challenging as the game itself.

Our tale begins in the Soviet Union, where a young software engineer, Alexey Pajitnov, created Tetris in 1984 while working at the Moscow Academy of Science. Pajitnov, inspired by a traditional puzzle game called Pentominoes, designed Tetris to be a game of mental challenge and abstract thinking. Unbeknownst to him, his creation would soon ignite a global frenzy.

Tetris quickly spread beyond the Iron Curtain, captivating players with its simple yet compelling gameplay. However, as the game's popularity surged, so did confusion over who held its rights. The Soviet Union, under its then-policy, claimed ownership of the game since Pajitnov was a government employee. But the specifics of international video game rights were murky, especially in an era when intellectual property laws varied dramatically between the Eastern and Western blocs.

Enter Henk Rogers, a Dutch video game designer and entrepreneur, who stumbled upon Tetris during a trade show in Las Vegas. Recognizing its potential, Rogers secured the rights to distribute Tetris on consoles in Japan. Meanwhile, in the United States, several companies, including giants like Nintendo and Atari, were also vying for a piece of the Tetris pie, each claiming they had legitimate rights to the game.

The legal labyrinth intensified when Nintendo launched its Game Boy system with Tetris as the flagship title. This move was a masterstroke in marketing, propelling both the Game Boy and Tetris to stratospheric success. However, it also escalated the legal war, with Atari (through its subsidiary Tengen) challenging Nintendo's claim to Tetris's console rights.

The ensuing legal battles were as intricate and fiercely contested as the game of Tetris itself. Courts in the United States and Japan were tasked with untangling the web of contracts, agreements, and claims over the game. In a pivotal ruling in 1989, a U.S. court sided with Nintendo, affirming their exclusive rights to Tetris on home video game consoles.

This verdict was a significant blow to Atari but a massive win for Nintendo, solidifying the Game Boy's dominance in the market. For Pajitnov, the game's creator, it was a bittersweet moment. While his creation had achieved global fame, he wouldn't see personal profits from it until years later, after the dissolution of the Soviet Union.

The Tetris rights dispute is a landmark case in the world of video games, highlighting the complexities of intellectual property in an increasingly globalized market. It's a tale of creativity caught in the crossfire of corporate giants, a reminder of the tangled paths innovations can take in their journey from a simple idea to a worldwide phenomenon.

19 - CRAZY LAWS OF ASIA

Singapore: Feeling free at home? In Singapore, walking around naked even in your own house can land you in hot water. Better keep those curtains drawn!

China: Family first in China! There's a law that requires adult children to visit their elderly parents regularly. Talk about legal family bonding!

Japan: Watch your waistline in Japan! The "Metabo Law" mandates yearly waist measurements for adults to encourage healthy living. Over the limit? Time for diet classes.

Bangladesh: Cheating on exams in Bangladesh is a serious offense. Students can find themselves behind bars for trying to outsmart their tests.

Thailand: Going commando in Thailand? Think again. It's illegal to leave your underwear at home. And watch where you step – disrespecting currency with the King's image by stepping on it could land you in trouble.

China: Reincarnation in China comes with a twist – it's illegal for Tibetan Buddhist monks to reincarnate without government permission. Talk about controlling the cycle of life and death!

India: Failed a suicide attempt in India? You could end up in jail. The law aims to deter such attempts but ends up penalizing the survivors.

South Korea: Night owls under 16 in South Korea have to log off online games by midnight. The "Cinderella Law" aims to curb video game addiction.

Malaysia: In Malaysia, cross-dressing is legally prohibited. The law focuses particularly on Muslim trans women, and it's used to justify their harassment, including physical and sexual assault.

Indonesia: Be careful if you plan on engaging in any romantic liaisons in Indonesia. Adultery is illegal here, and if you're caught, you could face some serious legal consequences.

Philippines: Fancy yourself as a bounty hunter? The Philippines is one of the few places where you can legally chase down fugitives for a reward. This echoes an old Wild West tradition, but with a modern twist.

Vietnam: In Vietnam, it's illegal to change a light bulb unless you're a licensed electrician. Seems like a bit of an overkill for such a mundane task, but it's the law!

Singapore: Singing in public with obscene lyrics is a big no in Singapore. If you're caught, you could face a fine or even imprisonment. Best to keep your karaoke songs clean!

Thailand: If you're a movie buff in Thailand, think twice before bringing a VCR home. The possession of more than 120 unlicensed video tapes or DVDs is illegal, a law likely aimed at curbing piracy.

Bhutan: Bhutan takes its environmental conservation seriously. It's mandated by law that at least 60% of the country must remain forested for all future generations. A beautiful commitment to nature, indeed.

20 - THE TERRIBLE SPLIT: A DIVORCE DRAMA OF PARTITIONED PROPERTIES

In the legal annals of the 1970s, amidst the disco and bell-bottoms, emerged a divorce case as peculiar as its name: Terrible v. Terrible. It's 1975, and the Supreme Court of Nevada is abuzz with a property dispute that sounds straight out of a sitcom. Enter Elizabeth and Joseph Terrible, a couple whose marriage dissolved four years earlier, leaving behind a medley of assets and a property entanglement worthy of a daytime drama.

The Terrible residence, once a symbol of marital unity, had become a battleground. During happier times, the Terribles held the property as "joint tenants," sharing equal rights. Post-divorce, the plot thickens as the property transforms into "tenants in common," with each Terrible holding a separate, undivided half-interest. A real estate plot twist, if there ever was one!

Cue to Joseph Terrible, who receives an offer to sell the property. He's ready to bid adieu to the past, but there's a catch – Elizabeth refuses the sale. In a move that would make any legal drama proud, Joseph files a case to partition his interest in the property. It's a legal labyrinth, with twists and turns of agreements and rights, enough to make anyone's head spin.

The court, in a decision dripping with the wisdom of Solomon, rules that Joseph cannot force a partition. Why? Because during their divorce saga, he had agreed to let Elizabeth manage the property until they both consented to a sale. Enter the hero of our story, equitable estoppel – a legal principle that's the equivalent of a stern parent, ensuring no one backs out of their promises.

In a ruling that's part legal brilliance, part matrimonial morality tale, the court holds that agreements made in the shadow of divorce have the staying power of superglue. The Terrible property saga ends not with a sale, but with a legal lesson in commitments and consequences.

"The Terrible Split" is more than a case; it's a narrative cocktail of legal intricacies and human drama, with a title that brings a smirk. It's a story that reminds us that in the theater of law, sometimes the name is as memorable as the tale itself.

21 - THE BATTLE
OF THE BEVERAGE

The early 2000s, a time of rapid technological innovation and fierce corporate competition, set the stage for a David vs. Goliath legal battle in the beverage industry: Juicy Whip, Inc. v. Orange Bang, Inc. Picture Juicy Whip, a relatively small player in the beverage game, accusing industry giant Orange Bang of patent infringement over a novel beverage-dispensing machine.

Orange Bang counters, challenging the very utility of Juicy Whip's patent. It's a high-stakes duel of wits and legal strategies, where the validity and enforcement of patents hang in the balance.
The court becomes an arena where evidence and arguments swirl like ingredients in a mixer.

Juicy Whip's claims are scrutinized, Orange Bang's counterarguments dissected. But in a twist of legal fate, the court finds that the evidence doesn't quite quench the thirst for proof needed to invalidate Juicy Whip's patent.

The verdict is reversed and remanded, a lifeline to Juicy Whip's claims, and a moment of reckoning for Orange Bang. The case becomes a hallmark in the beverage industry, not just for its legal outcome, but for the narrative it weaves around the complexities of patent law and corporate rivalry.

In the end, "The Battle of the Beverage Titans" serves up a concoction of legal intrigue, innovation, and the relentless pursuit of corporate victory, all set against the backdrop of the dynamic turn-of-the-century business world.

21 - THE GREAT CLACKER BALL CONUNDRUM: A LEGAL TALE OF 50,000 BOXES

The year 1976 witnessed a curious legal spectacle: the United States government versus 50,000 cardboard boxes, each containing a pair of clacker balls. These seemingly innocuous toys became the target of a federal lawsuit under the Federal Hazardous Substances Act. Dubbed dangerous for their potential to fragment and launch pieces hazardously, the clacker balls' fate hung in the balance.

In a courtroom drama reminiscent of David vs. Goliath, the government argued for the confiscation and destruction of these toys, claiming they posed a significant risk to public safety. The court, presiding over this unusual case, sided with the government, ruling that the clacker balls were indeed hazardous and therefore subject to seizure and destruction following their interstate journey.

This landmark case, unique in its focus on an object rather than an individual, highlighted the intricate and often unexpected intersections of consumer safety, legal responsibility, and government intervention. It stands as a testament to the era's growing awareness of product safety and the lengths to which the law would go to protect the public from hidden dangers in everyday items.

22. THE CASE OF THE WRONG FORECAST: WHEN RAIN DAMPENED A LAWSUIT

In the sun-drenched city of Tel Aviv, where perfect beach days seem almost guaranteed, a 2021 lawsuit cast a curious cloud over the usually predictable skies. The defendant? Not a rogue storm system, but the city's own beloved weatherman, Danny Rup. The plaintiff? A disgruntled resident who claimed Rup's sunny forecast led her astray, straight into a flu-filled puddle of misfortune.

The story goes like this: Our protagonist, an unnamed woman (let's call her Esther, because everyone deserves a little sunshine in their name), tuned in to Rup's weather report on Channel 2. Basking in the promise of clear skies, Esther shed her sensible raincoat and opted for a breezy summer dress. Unfortunately, Mother Nature had other plans, unleashing a downpour that would make a monsoon blush.

Esther, soaked to the bone and sporting a newfound chill, promptly fell ill with a nasty case of the flu. Missing a week of work and shelling out for medication, Esther's sunny disposition turned stormy. Fueled by sniffles and a sense of injustice, she decided to take legal action against the TV station and weatherman, Rup, for the sum of $1,000.

Esther's claim hinged on the argument that Rup's inaccurate forecast constituted professional negligence. By providing "false and misleading information," she argued, the TV station had essentially caused her illness and subsequent financial losses. The defense, predictably, countered that weather forecasting is an inherently inexact science, and holding weathermen accountable for every raindrop would be like suing a palm reader for a cloudy future.

The Israeli small claims court, however, sided with Esther. The judge, perhaps swayed by Esther's sniffles or convinced by the legal precedent of "wet negligence," ruled in her favor. Channel 2 was ordered to pay the $1,000 compensation, a small price to pay for a potentially precedent-setting lawsuit.

The "Wrong Forecast" case became a national curiosity, sparking debates about personal responsibility, the limits of legal claims, and the ever-fickle nature of the weather. While some saw it as a frivolous lawsuit, others viewed it as a David-and-Goliath win for the everyday citizen against the perceived infallibility of the media.

Esther, meanwhile, presumably enjoyed her flu-free victory (and perhaps a nice, sunny day at the beach) – a testament to the fact that sometimes, even the most unexpected lawsuits can bring a ray of sunshine into the courtroom.

While Esther's case may seem like a quirky one-off, it raises interesting questions about the legal boundaries of weather forecasting. Can weathermen be held liable for inaccurate predictions, especially if those predictions lead to personal injury or financial losses? The answer, as Esther's case shows, is not always clear-cut.

In most countries, weather forecasting is considered a form of free speech, protected by freedom of expression laws. However, there are instances where forecasters can be held accountable for negligence, such as if they knowingly issue false or misleading warnings. Ultimately, each case is judged on its own merits, and the line between a bad forecast and actionable negligence remains a hazy one. So, the next time you step out the door after checking the weather report, remember:

- Pack an umbrella, just in case.
- Don't blame the weatherman if you get caught in a downpour.
- And if you do decide to sue, be prepared for a potentially stormy legal battle.

After all, the weather, like the law, is never truly predictable. But one thing's for sure: even the most unexpected lawsuits can sometimes shed light on the often-murky relationship between sunshine, raindrops, and the pursuit of justice.

23 - CRAZY LAWS OF EUROPE

Europe's legal landscape isn't a single tapestry, but rather a quilt woven with threads of history, quirky traditions, and a dash of humor. Europe's patchwork of laws comes from centuries of independent kingdoms and evolving cultures. Think of it like a family recipe passed down for generations, each country adding its own secret ingredient (and occasionally forgetting a pinch of salt).

In Italy, the Roman emphasis on order and public decorum still echoes in laws like the anti-skirt rule and the mandatory smile (except when faced with life's lemons). In Switzerland, Sunday's tranquility is fiercely protected, even if it means silencing laundry lines and toilet flushes.

Cultural quirks take center stage: From Denmark's child-under-the-car check to Sweden's paint-license requirement, Europe isn't afraid to prioritize unique cultural values. These laws reflect a focus on safety, aesthetics, and preserving a certain way of life. Remember, Europe is home to countless towns bursting with history and charm, and sometimes, the laws bend to protect that special character.

Humor sometimes gets a seat at the table: Sure, Europe has its serious laws, but there's also a touch of whimsy woven in. France's "marry-a-dead-person" law stemmed from a real-life tragedy, but its wording adds a quirky twist. And who can deny the absurdity of Belgium's oxen-and-dog-powered-army-vehicles law? It's a reminder that even in the world of legalese, a little laugh can't hurt.

It's not just about individual states: Unlike the US with its separate federal and state laws, Europe has the European Union, where some rules apply across the continent. This adds another layer to the legal landscape, creating a blend of national quirks and EU-wide regulations. Think of it like a larger pot boiling over the national stoves, occasionally adding its own broth to the dish.

So, while the US legal system might be a streamlined highway, Europe's is a winding village road, full of unexpected turns and charming detours. It's a system shaped by history, culture, and a touch of eccentricity, which, let's be honest, makes it all the more fascinating. And hey, even if you can't wear a skirt in Milan or play music in a Finnish taxi, there's no denying that exploring Europe's legal quirks is an adventure in itself!

Italy: Men, be careful with your fashion choices in Italy. It's illegal for men to wear skirts. Also, in Milan, it's a legal requirement to always smile, except during funerals or hospital visits.

Switzerland: Late-night bathroom users, take note. In Switzerland, flushing the toilet in an apartment after 10 pm is considered illegal.

Sweden: Planning to give your house a fresh coat of paint? You'll need to get a license first. This law is designed to maintain aesthetic harmony, particularly within city bounds. Also, don't even think about posting a picture of Swedish Krona; it's protected by copyright.

Finland: Long taxi ride? Don't expect any background tunes. In Finland, playing music in a taxi without paying a copyright fee to the Finnish Composers Copyright Society is against the law.

Denmark: Before driving off, it's compulsory in Denmark to check under your car for children. This thorough pre-driving check is a unique legal requirement.

Netherlands: If a burglar breaks into your house, think twice before locking them in the bathroom. Depriving a burglar of their liberty, even when they're stealing your stuff, is against the law in the Netherlands.

Belgium: In a throwback to times of war, dogs and oxen can be requisitioned to propel army vehicles. This law, dating back to 1939, still exists in the Belgian military code.

Luxembourg: Driving a car without windshield wipers? That's illegal in Luxembourg, even if your car doesn't have a windshield!

Germany: Running out of fuel on the Autobahn is not just a travel faux pas; it's actually illegal. This law is in place because stopping on the highway for preventable reasons, like running out of fuel, is considered a hazard.

UK: Handling salmon in suspicious circumstances is actually against the law, as per the Salmon Act of 1986. This peculiar wording relates to illegal fishing activities.

France: In a rule that seems more storybook than legal code, it's legal to marry a dead person in France, provided there's evidence of plans to marry before their death. This law was introduced after a tragic incident in 1959.

Denmark: Before setting off in your car, you must check under it for children. This thorough check is a unique Danish legal requirement to ensure safety.

Portugal: Thinking of relieving yourself in the sea? Better think twice in Portugal, as it's illegal to pee in the ocean.

Netherlands: Surprisingly, it's against the law to lock a burglar in your toilet during a break-in. This law is centered on the principle of not depriving someone of their liberty, even if they are committing a crime.

Greece: High heels are banned at archeological sites in Greece. This is to prevent damage to these historically important locations.

Italy: In the Isle of Capri, wearing noisy sandals is a no-go. This law is aimed at maintaining a certain level of decorum in this picturesque location.

Switzerland: Be cautious when doing laundry on a Sunday. Hanging clothes out to dry is not allowed, reflecting the country's appreciation for tranquility on this day of rest.

Germany: It is legal to break out of prison, an interesting reflection of the country's legal perspective on the freedom of individuals.

Sweden: During the winter darkness period, it's illegal to complain about wishing it were sunny. This law reflects the country's approach to coping with its long, dark winters.

Austria: Don't get caught sleeping naked on a balcony in Austria. Public nudity, even in the comfort of your own home, is considered a disturbance of the peace.

Spain: In parts of Spain, chewing gum is a sticky situation. Some towns banned it due to concerns about litter and sidewalk cleanup. So, keep your chomping discreet!

Croatia: Feeling patriotic? Don't burn the Croatian flag, even unintentionally. This act of disrespect can land you in hot water.

Ireland: Public intoxication is no laughing matter in Ireland. Even walking under the influence can earn you a fine. So, pace yourself at the pub!

Iceland: Need a new hamster? Forget about it. Importing live hamsters to Iceland is strictly prohibited, aimed at protecting the island's fragile ecosystem.

Hungary: Forget singing along to Hungarian national ant in a public place, unless you're at a special ceremony. Belting it out casually can be seen as disrespectful.

Norway: Thinking of naming your child "Bob"? Not so fast in Norway. Naming authorities have the power to reject names they deem unfit, aiming for linguistic and cultural appropriateness.

Czech Republic: Feeling stressed? Don't scream in silence. In some Czech towns, making excessive noise after 10 pm, even indoors, can result in a fine. Respect those bedtime hours!

Scotland: It's against the law to be drunk and disorderly in a chargehouse, which is basically a drunk tank. Seems like a redundant rule, but apparently, things can get wild even in a holding cell.

Poland: Want to take a selfie with a pigeon? Think twice. Feeding or attracting wild pigeons in public spaces is prohibited in some Polish cities due to concerns about hygiene and nuisance.

Spain: In some Spanish towns, throwing bread on the ground is a no-no. Respecting food is a big deal, so treat those crusts with dignity!

France: Planning a picnic in the Palace of Versailles? Hold your horses (not literally, they're banned too!). Eating on the palace grounds is strictly forbidden.

Germany: Need to blow your nose in public? Do it quietly. Loudly honking your snot rocket is considered disruptive and rude.

Denmark: Don't even think about wearing slippers outside your house in Denmark. Shoes are mandatory for public appearances, even if you're just popping out for a quick stroll.

Italy: In Venice, feeding the pigeons is a bad idea. Not only is it messy, but the city has implemented hefty fines to deter feathered freeloaders.

Switzerland: If you're a dog owner in Switzerland, be prepared for some doggy duties. Leaving your pup's poop unbagged on the sidewalk is an offense punishable by a fine.

Netherlands: Want to go skinny dipping in Amsterdam? Think again. Public nudity is prohibited in most waterways and beaches, so keep your birthday suit private.

Finland: Need some new furniture? Building your own wooden chair? In Finland, you'll need a permit before you hammer away. This ensures construction aligns with aesthetic standards.

Sweden: Dying for a quick tan? Sunbathing on balconies in some Swedish cities is illegal. Apparently, soaking up rays in your undergarments can disturb the neighbours' peace.

Portugal: In Portugal, driving with flip-flops is a no-no. Safe footwear is mandatory for hitting the road, so ditch the beachy vibes for your driving adventures.

Greece: In some Greek islands, throwing confetti is strictly forbidden. Apparently, celebrating a bit too enthusiastically can lead to a tidy-up battle.

Ireland: Need to silence a noisy neighbour? Don't crank up the music in retaliation. Playing loud music between 11 pm and 8 am in Ireland can land you in legal trouble.

Austria: In Vienna, don't even think about painting your front door pink. Building regulations dictate specific colour palettes for different districts, so choose your hues wisely.

Belgium: Forget about using a leaf blower on Sundays in Belgium. Disturbing the peace with noisy tools is forbidden on the day of rest.

Luxembourg: Need to take a quick shower after a gym session? Be aware that in some Luxembourg towns, showering between 10 pm and 6 am is illegal. Apparently, late-night water usage is frowned upon.

Germany: In some German cities, walking across a red light after a pedestrian signal turns off is technically legal. However, proceed with caution, as jaywalking is still generally discouraged.

France: Planning a road trip? Make sure your car has two breathalyzers on board. In France, drivers are required to carry these devices in case of police checks.

Spain: Need to take a quick siesta? In some Spanish towns, closing stores for the afternoon siesta is mandatory. So, embrace the laid-back rhythm and join the snooze fest!

Norway: Don't wear camouflage clothing in Norway, especially near military installations. Blending in with the troops can be misconstrued as a security risk.

Czech Republic: Want to name your baby "Lucifer"? Not happening in the Czech Republic. Names deemed offensive or detrimental to the child's well-being are off the table.

24. WHEN LINGERIE LAUNCHED A LEGAL BRAWL

In the sun-kissed haven of Los Angeles, where dreams are spun from spun sugar and beach bodies glisten under a perpetual spotlight, a tale of undergarment-induced mayhem unfolded in the year 2008. Our heroine, let's call her Valerie (because every diva deserves a dramatic moniker), wasn't your average angel-winged shopper. No, Valerie, a traffic warden whose daily battles involved rogue double parkers and expired meters, harbored a secret yearning for a touch of Victoria's Secret magic.

So, there she was, bathed in the soft glow of a fitting room, about to slip into a pair of panties promising untold flirtatious victories. The fabric, oh so delicate, whispered promises of silken seduction. The rhinestones, oh so sparkly, winked like mischievous little conspirators. But little did Valerie know, one of those rhinestone rascals was harboring a mischievous glint of its own – a glint that would soon launch her into the dizzying orbit of a courtroom showdown.

With the grace of a gazelle on roller skates (and trust me, that's not graceful), the rhinestone, held captive by a treacherous metal clasp, decided to stage a daring escape. In a flash faster than a Victoria's Secret model changing outfits, it shot off like a rogue comet, aiming straight for Valerie's unsuspecting eye.

The ensuing scene was less runway strut and more slapstick opera. Valerie, clutching her throbbing eye and sporting a newfound appreciation for pirate patches, found herself staring at a world blurred with sparkly stars (the non-Victoria's Secret kind, unfortunately). But Valerie, a woman who wrangled renegade cars for a living, wasn't about to let a little rhinestone rebellion dim her inner diva.

Armed with an attorney fiercer than a leopard in stilettos, Valerie filed a lawsuit against the lingerie giant. The charges? Sudden rhinestone assault? Emotional distress induced by sparkly projectiles? Medical bills that could buy a lifetime supply of push-up bras? You betcha!

The courtroom became a stage for a legal tango of liability and responsibility. Experts pontificated on the perils of rogue embellishments, lawyers sparred like overzealous lingerie sales associates on commission, and the fate of Valerie's eye (and potential compensation) hung in the balance.

The verdict, shrouded in the secrecy of court settlements, remains a tantalizing mystery. Did Valerie's eye recover its sparkle? Did her bank account see a similar glint? The world may never know. But one thing is certain: the Case of the Renegade Rhinestone stands as a cautionary tale for both lingerie enthusiasts and manufacturers.

So, the next time you reach for that delicately lacy number, remember Valerie's tale. Approach those sparkly adornments with the skepticism of a seasoned diamond appraiser, and never underestimate the legal firepower of a wronged traffic warden with a rhinestone in her eye. After all, you never know when your quest for lingerie perfection might take a decidedly un-sexy legal turn.

And who knows, maybe your own tale of undergarment-induced mishaps will grace the pages of future trivia books, forever reminding the world that even the most glamorous garments can harbor hidden dangers, and that sometimes, the most unexpected heroes wear traffic warden uniforms and have a rhinestone-shaped chip on their shoulder.

25 - WHEN TOILETS TURNED TORPEDOES: THE FLUSHMATE III SAGA

In the porcelain palaces of American bathrooms, where privacy reigns and nature takes its course, a silent menace lurked unseen. The year was 2004, and the Flushmate III, a pressure-assisted toilet system promising a watery whoosh of efficiency, was quietly conquering suburban basements and master baths. Little did homeowners know, their gleaming thrones harbored a ticking time bomb, one primed to erupt in a shower of ceramic shrapnel and startled screams.

This wasn't your average case of plumbing mishap. No, the Flushmate III explosions, as they would come to be known, were fueled by a faulty pressure tank design. A small plastic seam, vulnerable to stress and corrosion, could give way at any moment, sending the tank's pressurized water shooting through the porcelain like a miniature cannon. The results were anything but charming: shattered toilets, flying debris, and, in some unfortunate cases, injuries ranging from cuts and bruises to broken bones and punctured ears.

One such victim was Gary, a burly construction worker from Ohio. As Gary settled into his morning ritual, the Flushmate III unleashed its fury. The tank exploded, showering him with shards of porcelain and a wave of icy water. Gary emerged with a gash on his leg and a newfound respect for the power of a malfunctioning toilet.

Gary's story was far from unique. Across the country, over 2 million Flushmate III toilets were installed in unsuspecting homes. And with each flush, the potential for disaster lurked. Reports trickled in: a housewife in Iowa narrowly escaping a porcelain shrapnel storm, a plumber in Florida wrestling with a geyser of toilet water, a family dog in California whimpering from a porcelain-induced earache.

Enough was enough. In 2009, a band of intrepid lawyers, armed with tales of shattered porcelain and shaken nerves, launched a class-action lawsuit against Sloan Valve, the Flushmate III's manufacturer. The courtroom became a battleground, with lawyers dissecting pressure gauges and engineers debating the tensile strength of plastic seams. The media, ever eager for a juicy scandal, dubbed it the "Explosive Bathroom Battle."

Finally, in 2016, justice flushed its way through the legal pipes. Sloan Valve agreed to a $18 million settlement, a sum awarded to the hundreds of injured parties and those whose porcelain thrones had met an untimely demise. Gary, our construction worker hero, walked away with a hefty compensation package and a healthy dose of skepticism towards toilets that promised more than just a simple flush.

The Flushmate III saga serves as a cautionary tale, a reminder that even the most mundane household objects can harbor hidden dangers. It's a testament to the power of collective action, of disgruntled homeowners and fearless lawyers joining forces to flush away injustice. And, perhaps most importantly, it's a hilarious, albeit slightly terrifying, reminder to always approach your morning throne with a healthy dose of respect – you never know what might erupt when you press that handle.

So, the next time you settle into your bathroom sanctuary, remember: the Flushmate III saga was real, and it reminds us that even in the most private of domains, danger can lurk, waiting to unleash a porcelain pandemonium. Proceed with caution, and flush responsibly. Your plumbing, and your sanity, will thank you.

26 - CASE OF THE VANISHING TROUSERS: WHEN DRY CLEANING BECAME A LEGAL ODYSSEY

In the bustling heart of Washington, D.C., where power suits rule the sartorial landscape, a sartorial saga unfolded in 2005 that would leave one man trouserless and the legal system grappling with the true cost of lost pants. Our protagonist, let's call him Arthur (because everyone deserves a dapper alias in a courtroom drama), entrusted his prized gray trousers to the seemingly innocuous clutches of Custom Cleaners. Little did he know, this seemingly routine dry-cleaning endeavor was about to morph into a legal odyssey wilder than any political scandal.

When Arthur returned, primed to reclaim his sartorial armor, he was met with a chilling truth: his pants had vanished. No rip, no stain, just a gaping hole in Custom Cleaners' inventory and a void in Arthur's wardrobe. Now, Arthur wasn't your average dry-cleaning patron. He was a man of principle, a legal eagle whose suits had seen the inside of courtrooms more often than the inside of a washing machine. So, what was a man of justice to do? Sue, of course. And sue big.

Arthur, channeling his inner David facing Goliath, aimed his legal slingshot at Custom Cleaners, demanding a staggering $54 million in compensation. His argument? Not just the tangible loss of his beloved trousers, but the intangible, soul-crushing burden of mental suffering. The "Satisfaction Guaranteed" sign emblazoned in the shop, he argued, was a binding contract, an ironclad pact between man and cleaner, promising sartorial bliss or financial apocalypse. The dry cleaners, naturally, scoffed. They countered that pants, alas, are not immune to the cruel whims of laundry fate, and that while they regretted the missing trousers, Arthur's astronomical claim bordered on the sartorial absurd.

The courtroom became a stage for a sartorial showdown. Lawyers sparred over the legal weight of dry-cleaning guarantees, psychologists pondered the true cost of trouser-induced distress, and fashion experts debated the finer points of gray wool slacks. The judge, bless his cotton socks, must have felt like he'd stumbled into a Kafkaesque nightmare populated by missing pants and million-dollar lawsuits.

In the end, justice, much like a well-tailored suit, demands a sense of proportion. While Arthur's case may have tickled the public's funny bone and challenged legal boundaries, the judge deemed his $54 million claim a tad excessive. In 2007, the gavel delivered its verdict: Custom Cleaners would not face financial ruin, and Arthur, though trouserless, was left with a lighter legal burden and a valuable lesson in the limitations of dry-cleaning warranties.

The Case of the Vanishing Trousers, while ultimately a footnote in legal history, stands as a testament to the human capacity for creative litigation and the sartorial importance of a good pair of pants. It reminds us that while lost clothing may indeed cause distress, the price tag on such suffering should, perhaps, remain within the realm of reason. So, the next time you entrust your garments to the mysterious world of dry cleaning, remember Arthur's tale. Embrace the potential for sartorial mishaps with a chuckle, but keep your legal demands firmly rooted in the realm of reality. After all, even in the world of high-stakes laundry, sanity (and a well-stocked wardrobe) should always trump the allure of a million-dollar lawsuit.

27 - THE LION STRIKES BACK: WHEN SAFARI WENT SAVAGE AND LEGAL

In the sun-baked savannas of Africa, where the primal echoes of nature reverberate through ancient acacia trees, a tale unfolded in 2007 that blurred the lines between predator and prey, hunter and hunted. Our protagonist, not your average nature photographer, was a big-game hunter named Thomas Caldwell. In his sights: a magnificent lion, a king of the jungle poised to become a trophy on Caldwell's wall.

But the story, as these often do, took a dramatic turn. As Caldwell fired his weapon, aiming for the lion's shoulder, the bullet, instead of delivering a merciful kill, merely grazed the beast. Enraged and wounded, the lion lunged forward, transforming Caldwell from hunter to the hunted. The savanna became a battleground, and when the dust settled, it was Caldwell – not the lion – lying bloodied and mauled.

Battered and bewildered, Caldwell sought a peculiar form of justice. He filed a lawsuit against Federal Cartridge Co., the manufacturer of the bullet that failed him in his moment of need. His argument? The ammunition, he claimed, was defective, its supposed stopping power a cruel illusion that led him to be savaged by his intended prey. The courtroom became a fascinating stage for a legal duel unlike any other. Experts dissected ballistics and hunting methods, lawyers sparred over the inherent risks of big-game hunting, and the presiding judge must have felt like he was navigating a legal jungle as wild as the one where the attack occurred.

Ultimately, the court dismissed Caldwell's case. The ruling, while acknowledging the unfortunate turn of events, pointed to the inherent unpredictability of hunting, the risks that every big-game hunter accepts when stepping into the lion's domain. Federal Cartridge Co.'s bullet, the court concluded, while perhaps not achieving the desired kill, had performed within its expected parameters.

The tale of Thomas Caldwell serves as a stark reminder that in the natural world, even the best-laid plans can be undone by the untamed forces of nature. It's a cautionary tale for big-game hunters, a legal precedent that underscores the inherent risks of confronting apex predators, and a testament to the surprising ways in which the tables can turn in the wild dance between hunter and hunted.

So, the next time you gaze upon a majestic lion in its natural habitat, remember Caldwell's story. Embrace the awe-inspiring power of nature, but never underestimate its potential for violence. And if you choose to venture into the lion's domain, do so with the utmost respect and the sobering awareness that sometimes, the hunter becomes the prey, and the only justice delivered is the roar of the wild itself.

28 - THE TALE OF THE LOST SHEEP AND A ONE-DOLLAR VERDICT

On the rolling hills of Massachusetts, where sheep graze lazily amongst apple orchards and weathered barns, a tale unfolded in 2008 that would pit neighbor against neighbor and turn bleating companionship into a bleating legal battle. Our protagonists, let's call them the Shepherds (because everyone deserves a pastoral alias in a livestock-related drama), were a couple whose hearts found solace in the woolly company of their beloved sheep.

But their idyllic farm life took a tragic turn when their canine neighbors, a pack of rambunctious hounds, launched a predatory raid on the unsuspecting sheep. The aftermath was bleatingly grim: seven sheep lost, the Shepherds heartbroken, and a chasm of distrust opening up between them and their dog-owning neighbors.

Unable to let the woolly woefulness go, the Shepherds, channeling their inner David against Goliath, decided to take their grief to court. They aimed for the financial jugular, demanding a staggering $140,000 in compensation for their emotional distress and the loss of their furry companions. The legal argument? Their sheep, they claimed, were more than just livestock; they were family, their soft baas a balm to the soul, their fleeces a warm embrace against the Massachusetts chill.

The courtroom became a stage for a barnyard-esque legal squabble. Lawyers grappled with the monetary value of sheep-induced emotional well-being, experts pontificated on the emotional depth of ovine companions, and the judge must have felt like he'd stumbled into a bizarre cross between Mr. McGregor's garden and a Perry Mason courtroom.

Ultimately, the Shepherds' legal gambit stumbled like a newborn lamb on wobbly legs. The court, while acknowledging the emotional toll of losing livestock, balked at the astronomical sum demanded. Instead, they ordered the Shepherds to produce concrete evidence of their sheep's worth – receipts, market evaluations, anything to quantify the loss beyond bleating anecdotes.

But here's where the story takes a truly comedic turn. The Shepherds, perhaps clinging to the intangible value of their woolly companions, refused to cooperate. They wouldn't, or couldn't, provide any evidence of their sheep's market worth. So, in a legal twist worthy of a slapstick farmhand routine, the judge, left with no choice, awarded the Shepherds the grand sum of… one dollar.

The Case of the Lost Sheep, while ultimately a footnote in legal history, stands as a testament to the human capacity for creative litigation, the emotional attachment we form with our four-legged (or, in this case, four-footed) companions, and the importance of evidence when bleating for legal justice. So, the next time you gaze upon a grazing sheep, remember the Shepherds' tale. Embrace the fuzzy joy of farmyard friendships, but keep your legal demands grounded in the realm of the demonstrably quantifiable. After all, even in the court of animal affection, one dollar for a lost sheep may be all the wooly justice you get.

29 - WHEN TEXTING TURNED TURBULENT ON A DATE

In the sun-drenched streets of Austin, Texas, where quirky bars and live music hum beneath a perpetual blue sky, a tale unfolded in 2017 that would pit etiquette against convenience, and a movie date against the perils of the ever-present phone. Our protagonist, let's call him Maverick (because even a courtroom drama deserves a touch of Texas swagger), ventured out for a cinematic rendezvous with an unnamed date. Unfortunately, the only galaxy they encountered wasn't in the "Guardians of the Galaxy Vol. 2" playing on screen, but rather the constellation of notifications lighting up his date's phone.

As minutes morphed into a textually-tantalizing eternity, Maverick, a self-proclaimed movie maven, felt his enjoyment of the spacefaring action steadily draining away. He attempted a diplomatic intervention, a gentle nudge towards the cinematic spectacle unfolding before them. But alas, the siren song of the smartphone proved too alluring. Fueled by a potent cocktail of movie-snobbery and bruised ego, Maverick decided to take his grievance beyond the darkened confines of the theater. He filed a lawsuit against his date, demanding the princely sum of $17.31 – the cost of his ticket. His argument? Not just personal affront, but a violation of theater etiquette and a blatant disregard for the sacred art of movie-watching.

The legal world, ever eager for a juicy scandal, devoured the story. News outlets dubbed him "The Texting Terminator," late-night comedians poked fun at his cinematic crusade, and social media erupted in debates about phone etiquette and the sanctity of dates. Amidst the digital din, something curious happened. Maverick's date, likely weary of the media spotlight and perhaps harboring a touch of movie-watching remorse, offered a compromise. She would reimburse him for his ticket, on one condition: he leave her alone.

The Case of the Texting Date, while seemingly trivial, stands as a reminder of the ever-present battle between real-world experiences and the tempting glow of our digital devices. It reminds us that even on a date, amidst the promise of sparks and conversation, the allure of the smartphone can become a formidable villain. So, the next time you venture out for a cinema rendezvous, remember Maverick's tale.

Embrace the shared experience of the silver screen, put your phone on silent, and let the Guardians of the Galaxy (and hopefully, your date) have their rightful place in the spotlight. After all, a good movie, like a good date, deserves our undivided attention. And who knows, you might just avoid your own brush with the Texting Terminator, and walk away with a story worth sharing, not suing over.

30 - RED BULL'S WINGS CLIPPED: WHEN BUZZWORDS BACKFIRED

In the high-octane world of energy drinks, where marketing muscles flex as fiercely as biceps, Red Bull once reigned supreme. Their slogan, "Red Bull gives you wings," pulsed with audacious promises of superhuman energy and mental prowess. But as with any lofty flight, even the mightiest marketing wings can encounter turbulence. Enter 2014, and the year Red Bull's slogan came crashing down to earth, courtesy of a class-action lawsuit fueled by disgruntled consumers and the sharp eyes of eagle-eyed lawyers.

The plaintiffs, feeling deceived by the "wings" promise, argued that Red Bull lacked scientific evidence to substantiate its claims of enhanced focus and mental clarity. They weren't asking for literal wings, mind you, just a more grounded reality, a guarantee that their hard-earned dollars weren't buying empty hype. The courtroom became a battleground of caffeine molecules and buzzwords, where lawyers sparred over the legal weight of figurative language and the elusive science of focus.

Red Bull, initially defiant, soon realized their marketing wings were getting clipped. Facing potential damages that could make even an energy bull wince, they opted for a strategic landing: a $640,000 settlement. While not admitting any wrongdoing, they agreed to provide consumers with vouchers for Red Bull products or cash reimbursements.

The Case of the Clipped Wings serves as a cautionary tale for brands who soar too close to the sun of hyperbole. It reminds us that consumers, no longer content with simply buying into catchy slogans, are increasingly demanding transparency and substance. So, the next time you reach for a can of any beverage, be it energy-charged or not, remember Red Bull's tale.

Look beyond the flashy ads and buzzwords, and seek out products that stand on their own merits, without the need for borrowed wings. After all, true refreshment comes not from fleeting promises of superhuman feats, but from genuine quality and a healthy dose of skepticism.

And who knows, with a bit of critical thinking and a discerning palate, you might just discover your own inner superpower: the ability to choose wisely and fuel your day with products that live up to their claims, one grounded sip at a time.

31 - CRAZY LAWS OF THE UNITED STATES

Buckle up, because we're diving into the gloriously wacky world of American laws! It's true, the USA has a legal landscape as vast and diverse as the Grand Canyon itself. From coast to coast, state to state, there's a whole smorgasbord of rules and regulations, some sensible, some downright strange. Why is it like this? Well, grab your metaphorical cowboy hat and mosey on over, partner, because I'm about to lasso the reasons why American laws are such a tangled mess of fascinating contradictions.

Firstly, gotta remember the whole "50 independent states" thing. Each state is like its own miniature country, with its own history, culture, and, yes, you guessed it, laws. It's like a patchwork quilt sewn together with legal thread, each state adding its own unique squares of regulations. Want to sing karaoke before noon in Massachusetts? Nope, sorry, gotta wait till the afternoon sun shines. But head over to Nevada, and you can belt out your ballads before breakfast (just don't do it in your pajamas!).

Then there's the layer cake of federal law on top. Uncle Sam, bless his bureaucratic heart, has his own set of rules that apply to the whole shebang. Think taxes, national parks, and those fancy interstate highways you zoom down. So, sometimes state laws and federal laws play nice together, like two kids sharing a sandbox. But other times, they clash like cowboys over a water hole. Imagine California's love for environmental regulations bumping heads with Texas' oil industry. Sparks fly, legal battles ensue, and everyone gets a headache.

Another reason for the legal hodgepodge is the good ol' American spirit of innovation. We're a nation of pioneers, always pushing the boundaries, even when it comes to laws. Remember the Wild West days? Laws were practically scribbled on saloon napkins back then. As society evolved, so did the rules, leading to a sometimes messy, always interesting patchwork of legal precedents.

Think of it like a legal jazz solo, improvised on the fly, with each judge adding their own riff.

And let's not forget the influence of special interests and lobbyists. They're like the backroom dealers of the legal world, whispering sweet nothings (and maybe a few bucks) into the ears of politicians. This can lead to some pretty peculiar laws, like the one in Alabama that makes it illegal to sell peanuts after sundown (seriously, no late-night peanut cravings allowed!).

So, there you have it, folks. The reasons for America's vast and varied legal landscape are as complex and colorful as the country itself. It's a crazy quilt of history, culture, and good ol' American ingenuity, all stitched together with legal thread. And hey, even if it makes your head spin sometimes, there's no denying it's one heck of a ride. Now, go forth and explore the weird and wonderful world of American laws, partner. Just remember, don't wear pajamas while gambling in Nevada, and don't throw snowballs at cops in Missouri. You wouldn't want to end up on the wrong side of a legal hootenanny, now would you?

Wyoming: Skiers, think twice before hitting the slopes after a few drinks. It's illegal to ski while intoxicated in Wyoming, a law that makes perfect sense when you consider the safety aspects.

Louisiana: Love crawfish? In Louisiana, stealing these little crustaceans is a serious offense, with potential jail time for those who pinch too many.

Rockville, Maryland: Mind your language in Rockville. Public swearing can hit your wallet with a fine, keeping the streets family-friendly.

Gainesville, Georgia: Fried chicken enthusiasts, remember: in Gainesville, this poultry delight must be eaten with your hands. Using utensils is not just frowned upon, it's against the law!

Florida: Thinking of donning a mask for a midnight stroll? Not so fast. In Florida, adults roaming the streets masked can face legal repercussions, unless it's a holiday or a drill.

Rehoboth Beach, Delaware: If you're in church in Rehoboth Beach, keep those whispers to a minimum. Even a hushed conversation can be considered a disturbance and might attract a fine.

Hawaii: Here's an odd one – putting coins in your ears is a no-no in Hawaii. This law dates back to a time when the local currency was being destroyed, and people got creative with hiding their money.

Alabama: Driving blindfolded in Alabama? That's a definite no. Visibility is key when you're behind the wheel, and this law ensures drivers keep their eyes on the road.

Louisiana: Think sending a surprise pizza is a harmless prank? In Louisiana, it's considered harassment, and you might end up paying more than just for the pizza.

North Carolina: Bingo lovers, take note. In North Carolina, keep your bingo games under five hours, and stay sober while playing – both are the law.

Arkansas: Love your late-night snacks? Be careful in Arkansas, where it's illegal to honk your horn near a sandwich shop after 9 p.m. This law was likely enacted to prevent disturbances in dining areas.

Alabama: In Alabama, opening an umbrella on the street is prohibited. This unusual law might have been intended to prevent accidents or obstructions on crowded walkways.

Colorado: In Colorado, collecting rainwater is illegal. This law is likely tied to water rights and the allocation of natural resources.

Connecticut: A pickle must bounce to officially be considered a pickle in Connecticut. This peculiar standard was likely established to ensure the quality and texture of this popular snack.

Florida: Skateboarding without a license is prohibited in certain parts of Florida, reflecting an attempt to regulate this activity and ensure safety.

Georgia: In Quitman, Georgia, chickens are not permitted to cross the road. This law is likely a humorous take on ensuring livestock and poultry are kept under control.

Hawaii: It's against the law in Hawaii to place a coin behind your ear. This unique regulation dates back to early 20th-century efforts to control local currency.

Indiana: In Indiana, pi is legally 4, not 3.1415. This bizarre law appears to be a misunderstood attempt to simplify mathematics.

Kansas: It's illegal to catch a fish with bare hands in Kansas. This law might be aimed at protecting fish populations or ensuring fair sportsmanship in fishing.

Alabama: Selling peanuts after sundown is a no-go in some Alabama towns. This curious law may stem from concerns about food spoilage or sanitation in the pre-refrigeration era.

Arizona: It's illegal to hunt camels in Arizona, a seemingly unnecessary rule considering the rarity of wild camels in the state. This law likely arose from a failed experiment of using camels for transportation in the 19th century.

Colorado: If you're a dog owner in Denver, Colorado, don't expect to stroll through the park with more than two furry companions. This leash law limits the number of dogs one person can walk at a time.

Florida: In Key West, it's illegal to feed pigeons in public. This rule likely aims to control the pigeon population and keep beaches and tourist spots clean.

Illinois: In Chicago, wearing slippers while driving is forbidden. While the reason may seem unclear, it might be related to safety concerns regarding footwear that could potentially hinder proper control of the vehicle.

Maine: Forget using fireworks to celebrate, as they're generally illegal in most Maine towns and cities. This regulation aims to prevent fires and injuries associated with personal fireworks displays.

Nevada: In Elko County, Nevada, brothels are required to post a prominent sign with the words "No Loitering" clearly visible. This odd directive seems like a tongue-in-cheek attempt to maintain some semblance of decorum outside these establishments.

New Jersey: In Salem County, New Jersey, it's illegal to sing on Sundays except in church or at home. This antiquated law likely reflects strict religious observance of the Sabbath in past eras.

New York: Public swimming pools in New York City must have at least one lifeguard who can speak Yiddish. This requirement ensures the safety of Yiddish-speaking residents who may not understand English instructions during emergencies.

Oregon: In Baker County, Oregon, it's illegal to sell or purchase a live octopus. This rule is likely aimed at protecting octopus populations and preventing cruelty to these intelligent creatures.

Alabama: No fortune telling allowed except for entertainment purposes. So, predicting your future is okay for fun, but not if you're serious about it.

California: Unlawful to sell a baby doll without eyelashes within the state. Apparently, bald-eyed dolls are too creepy for Californians.

Florida: Live Oak trees are considered the State Tree, and it's illegal to kill or damage them without a permit. Guess Florida prefers leafy giants over sprawl.

Georgia: While masks are generally frowned upon, it's legal to wear one while riding a motorcycle... just to protect your face from bugs, of course.

Idaho: Throwing a brick at a highway is a big no-no, even if you have the world's strongest arm.

Illinois: If you're a barber in Chicago, don't even think about cutting hair on Sundays. Those locks will have to wait until Monday.

Kentucky: Dueling is technically legal, but only if both parties are registered blood donors and the fight takes place within 20 feet of a courthouse. Talk about a morbid twist on conflict resolution.

Louisiana: Throwing a banana peel in front of someone can land you in hot water. Seems slipping on potassium is considered assault in the Bayou State.

Massachusetts: In Nantucket, singing karaoke before noon is prohibited. So, save your belting for the afternoon crowds.

Michigan: Want to name your kid something wacky like "Strawberry Shortcake"? Prepare to get creative, as unusual names require court approval.

Minnesota: It's illegal to fish while sitting on a horse. Apparently, Minnesota prefers two-legged anglers.

Mississippi: Sunday shopping is a no-go in some counties, forcing residents to plan their purchases well in advance.

Missouri: Throwing snowballs at police officers is considered disorderly conduct. Even in a snowball fight, respect the blue.

Montana: Don't even think about selling used mattresses unless they're properly disinfected. No one wants to inherit someone else's nightmares (or bed bugs).

Nevada: While gambling is legal in Vegas, it's illegal to play slot machines while you're wearing pajamas. Dress code applies even to one-armed bandits.

New Hampshire: Don't try to bribe Santa Claus in New Hampshire. It's a misdemeanor, and who wants to be on the naughty list?

New Jersey: It's illegal to pump your own gas. So, sit back, relax, and let the professionals handle it.

New Mexico: Want to ride a camel? Head to New Mexico, where it's perfectly legal (unlike in neighboring Arizona).

New York: In New York City, it's illegal to shake a dust mop out your window. Imagine the chaos if everyone went on a spontaneous dusting spree!

Ohio: Selling goldfish in bowls smaller than one gallon is forbidden. Goldfish deserve some swimming space, even in the Buckeye State.

32 - THE BEAUTY TRAP: WHEN LOVE MET LEGAL DECEPTION

Unfolding in 2010 that would cast a chilling shadow on the notion of true love and blur the lines between beauty and deception. Our protagonist, Jian Feng, dreamt of a picture-perfect life – a beautiful wife, a perfect family, and a harmonious blend of modern ambition and ancestral respect. He found his vision seemingly embodied in Li, a woman whose stunning face and delicate grace whispered promises of eternal bliss.

Alas, the fairytale soon fractured into a legal nightmare. Upon the arrival of their newborn daughter, a jarring discordance shattered Jian's idyllic dreams. The baby, to his dismay, was "incredibly ugly," he claimed, bearing no resemblance to the delicate beauty he'd adored in Li. Accusations of infidelity flew, shattering the trust that had once bound them.

Li, cornered and desperate, revealed a hidden truth – a clandestine past sculpted by the knife of cosmetic surgery. Before meeting Jian, she had undergone extensive procedures, molding her features into the image of ethereal perfection that had captivated him. This revelation, instead of sparking understanding, ignited Jian's fury. He saw not just a concealed truth, but a calculated deception, a web of lies woven with surgical thread.

Driven by betrayal and the sting of shattered expectations, Jian took the unthinkable step. He embarked on a legal odyssey, accusing Li of "false pretenses" and demanding compensation for the life he felt he'd been misled into. The courtroom became a spectacle, a battleground where concepts of beauty, love, and the very definition of truth clashed spectacularly.

In a controversial verdict, the court sided with Jian. Li, deemed guilty of a calculated deception, was ordered to pay a staggering sum of over $120,000 – a price tag for the intangible loss of Jian's dream life. The news reverberated across China, igniting heated debates about the ethics of cosmetic surgery, the fragility of love based solely on physical appearance, and the legal implications of a beauty built on artifice.

The Case of the Ugly Baby stands as a stark reminder of the pitfalls of a society obsessed with physical perfection. It underscores the importance of honesty and transparency in relationships, and the dangers of mistaking fleeting beauty for genuine connection. It's a cautionary tale against succumbing to societal pressures and prioritizing appearances over the deeper wellsprings of love, trust, and acceptance.

33 - WHEN SLUMBER MET LAWSUIT: THE TALE OF A SLAMMING DESK AND A DISMISSED CLAIM

In the hallowed halls of Danbury High School, where knowledge supposedly reigns supreme, a sleepy student named Vinicios Robacher found himself at the center of a legal tussle that would raise eyebrows and test the limits of classroom etiquette. Our protagonist, Vinicios, wasn't known for his mathematical prowess, but rather for his impressive ability to catch forty winks during even the most riveting Pythagorean theorem discussions.

One fateful day, however, slumber collided with discipline when Vinicios' math teacher, seeking to awaken his mathematical muse, resorted to a somewhat drastic measure: a resounding desk slam. Alas, the intended pedagogical shockwave produced an unintended consequence – Vinicios claimed the slam, fueled by pedagogical zeal, resulted in hearing loss.

His parents, understandably alarmed, donned the armor of legal protection and launched a lawsuit against the school, the school board, and the entire city, presumably hoping to make them hear the injustice of their son's alleged sonic misfortune. The courtroom became a stage for a bizarre legal ballet, where lawyers pirouetted between decibel charts and educational methodologies, all while the judge must have felt like he'd stumbled into a Kafkaesque nightmare where a desk slam could land you in legal purgatory.

Ultimately, the court, unlike Vinicios in math class, remained wide awake to the legal nuances of the case. They deemed the desk slam, while perhaps jarring, a reasonable albeit unconventional attempt to rekindle Vinicios' mathematical spark. The lawsuit, after a valiant but ultimately futile legal slumber party, was dismissed.

The Case of the Sleeping Student and the Slamming Desk serves as a reminder that classrooms, while ostensibly bastions of learning, can occasionally become the breeding grounds for unexpected legal tangles. It highlights the delicate balance between maintaining classroom focus and respecting student well-being. It also reminds us that the law, like a vigilant teacher, always keeps its eyes (and ears) peeled for the line between discipline and potential liability.

So, the next time you find yourself nodding off during a particularly dry lecture, remember Vinicios' tale. Embrace the power of a good nap, but be aware that even the gentlest slumber can have unforeseen consequences. And for you, teachers, a gentle nudge or a well-placed question might be a safer (and less legally fraught) way to reawaken the slumbering muse within your students. After all, knowledge, unlike Vinicios' hearing, should never be a casualty in the quest for classroom engagement.

34 - WHEN RIDESHARES TURNED RELATIONSHIPS ROCKY: THE UNSETTLED SAGA OF UBER AND MARITAL MISHAPS

In the bustling streets of Paris, where romance whispers under the Eiffel Tower and espresso fuels late-night conversations, a tale unfolded in 2017 that would weave together the convenience of ridesharing with the tangled threads of marital trust. Our protagonist, a French businessman whose name remains shrouded in the fog of legal discretion, found himself at the center of a digital storm brewing within the Uber app.

Borrowing his wife's phone for a quick ride, our businessman, let's call him Monsieur X, logged into the Uber app, unaware of the digital gremlins lurking within. He completed his trip, blissfully oblivious to the glitch that lurked, a technological phantom ready to play havoc with his marital bliss.

That little gremlin, it seems, had a mischievous streak. Even after Monsieur X logged off, the app, possessed by its glitchy whims, continued to send his whereabouts directly to his wife's phone. Notifications pulsed with his movements, each ping a tiny digital tremor shaking the foundations of their trust.

Needless to say, Mrs. X, upon discovering this phantom trail of her husband's Uber journeys, wasn't thrilled. Suspicions blossomed like stubborn weeds, doubts bloomed like poisonous flowers, and Monsieur X found himself facing a storm of marital discord the likes of which no surge pricing could alleviate.

The tale escalated further when our aggrieved Monsieur X, channeling his entrepreneurial spirit, decided to take Uber to court. His argument? The app's glitch, he claimed, had played a significant role in the dissolution of his marriage, costing him not just his wife's trust, but a staggering $48 million in emotional damages.

The courtroom became a stage for a bizarre legal ballet, where lawyers tangoed between privacy violations and the weight of digital hiccups on marital harmony. Experts dissected app functions, psychologists pondered the fragility of trust in the age of geolocation, and the judge must have felt like he'd stumbled into a tech-infused episode of "Judge Judy."

The fate of Monsieur X's lawsuit, however, remains shrouded in the Parisian mist. No final verdict has been announced, leaving the story dangling like a half-downloaded Uber trip. Some whisper of settlements reached discreetly, others speculate on technical complexities that rendered the case untenable.

The Case of the Glitchy Uber and the Ruined Marriage, whether settled or still in legal limbo, stands as a cautionary tale for the digital age. It reminds us that technology, despite its intended conveniences, can sometimes become a mischievous accomplice in marital misunderstandings. It highlights the importance of communication and transparency, especially when our digital footprints trace paths that might raise eyebrows or fuel suspicions.

So, the next time you hail a ride on your mobile, remember Monsieur X's predicament. Embrace the ease of ridesharing, but safeguard your privacy, both digital and personal. And for those navigating the delicate terrain of marriage, remember, open communication is always the best app for building trust, far more reliable than any algorithm or even the most glitch-free ridesharing platform. After all, a happy marriage, unlike an Uber ride, should never depend on the whims of a digital gremlin.

35 - CRAZY LAWS OF THE MIDDLE EAST

From sandcastle regulations to goldfish rights, the Middle East offers a fascinating glimpse into a diverse legal landscape, where ancient traditions mingle with modern realities. So, ditch the guidebooks and prepare for a hilarious (and surprisingly informative) journey through laws that will make you scratch your head and chuckle in equal measure.

Privacy Palaces and Public Polishing: In the United Arab Emirates, your car is your kingdom, but keep it spick and span! A dusty chariot earns frowns and fines, while the thought of using a VPN for a sneaky peek at Netflix? Forget it! Privacy comes at a hefty price tag, literally. But fear not, fellow adventurers, for Dubai offers its own brand of thrills. Just keep your shimmying and salsa steps confined to your living room during Ramadan, because public dancing, even in the privacy of your own four walls, can land you in hot water.

Melodies and Misdemeanors: Music lovers, take note! Iran frowns upon public displays of Western tunes, so keep your head-banging for heavy metal confined to your headphones. In Saudi Arabia, Valentine's Day is celebrated with a subtle whisper, not a booming proclamation. Ditch the red roses and heart-shaped balloons, because even a splash of scarlet in your shop window could earn you a stern reprimand.

Snacking and Snapping: Got a rumble in your tummy on the Qatari bus? Quell it with a silent prayer, because public munching is a major faux pas. In Kuwait, watch your vocabulary, even in the digital realm. A keyboard-fueled tirade on WhatsApp could lead to real-world consequences. And in Bahrain, remember, a picture is not always worth a thousand words. Respecting privacy is paramount, so capture the scenery, not the faces.

United Arab Emirates: Planning to use a VPN in the UAE? Better think twice! It's not just about bypassing geo-blocks for your favorite show; you could be fined up to 2 million dirhams. That's a lot of money for a bit of extra browsing privacy! And about your car – keep it clean. A dusty car isn't just an eyesore; it's a ticket to finesville. Sandstorm or not, a dirty car is a no-go.

Dubai: Curiosity killed the cat, and in Dubai, snooping on someone's phone could kill your bank account. If you're caught peeking at someone else's phone without permission, you could face a hefty fine or a six-month vacation behind bars. Also, during Ramadan, keep the volume down. Dancing in your living room? Only if you can do it silently!

Iran: Feel like grooving to some Western tunes in Iran? You might want to stick to head-bopping in private. Public dancing, especially to Western music, could land you in more trouble than a bad dance move.

Saudi Arabia: In Saudi Arabia, Valentine's Day is less about hearts and flowers and more about keeping it low-key. Selling anything red or heart-shaped can be a heartbreaker for shop owners, as it goes against cultural norms. So, if you're feeling romantic, maybe stick to chocolates and a nice dinner inside.

Kuwait: In Kuwait, beware of bad language. Swearing on WhatsApp or other social media platforms isn't just rude, it's illegal. A digital slip of the tongue could land you in legal hot water.

Qatar: Fancy a quick snack on public transport in Qatar? Better hold that thought. Eating or drinking on buses, trains, and metros is a strict no-no. Getting caught mid-bite or sip might cost you more than the price of your snack.

Bahrain: In Bahrain, the personal is private, especially when it comes to photographs. Taking pictures of people without their explicit consent is not just a breach of social etiquette but a legal offense that can lead to serious consequences.

Oman: In Oman, keep an eye on your car's cleanliness. Much like in the UAE, a car that's not kept clean is not just seen as untidy but as a public nuisance, and could see you fined.

Lebanon: Love your pet fish in Lebanon? Make sure it's not a goldfish in a bowl. Oddly enough, keeping a goldfish in a bowl is considered animal cruelty due to the lack of space and stimulation.

Jordan: Thinking of borrowing a library book in Jordan? Just make sure to return it on time. Not returning library books is taken seriously and could see you facing more than just a late fee.

Israel: In Israel, picking up or collecting certain types of sea shells is prohibited, as they're considered a natural resource. So, beachcombers, look but don't take!
Turkey: Feeling fancy? Save the feather boas for another occasion. In Turkey, wearing overly flamboyant clothing in religious sites is considered disrespectful. Pack your travel wardrobe with tasteful attire instead.

Egypt: Craving a refreshing dip in the Red Sea? Remember, public nudity is strictly forbidden, even on secluded beaches. Opt for a swimsuit that keeps things covered for a swim without the worry.

Morocco: Calling all photographers! While capturing the beauty of Morocco is encouraged, snapping pictures of locals without their permission can land you in hot water. Respect their privacy and ask for consent before clicking that shutter.
Yemen: Feeling chatty on the phone? Keep your conversations in check when using public transportation in Yemen. Loud phone calls can be disruptive and disrespectful to fellow passengers.

Abu Dhabi: Got a sweet tooth? Think twice before chewing gum in Abu Dhabi. Importing, selling, or chewing gum is illegal for hygiene and environmental reasons. Stick to mints or candies instead.

Jordan: Planning a road trip? Buckle up and keep your hands on the wheel. Eating or drinking while driving is a no-go in Jordan, and police take road safety seriously. Focus on the road and enjoy the scenery later.

Israel: Feeling spontaneous? Resist the urge to climb ancient ruins. Touching and climbing historical structures in Israel is prohibited to prevent damage to these irreplaceable treasures. Appreciate them from afar.

Oman: Feeling adventurous? Think twice before venturing into the desert alone. Hiring a licensed guide is mandatory for desert excursions in Oman, ensuring your safety and respecting the delicate ecosystem.

Qatar: Love animals? Leave wild creatures alone. Feeding or approaching wild animals in Qatar, even with good intentions, can disrupt their natural behavior and potentially pose a danger. Observe them from a safe distance.

Saudi Arabia: Planning a pilgrimage to Mecca? Remember, public displays of affection, even between spouses, are not permitted in holy sites. Respecting local customs and religious sensitivities is paramount.

Iran: Feeling artistic? Public graffiti is a no-no in Iran. Expressing yourself creatively is encouraged, but stick to designated spaces and avoid defacing public property.

United Arab Emirates: Don't let the glitz and glamour fool you. Public drunkenness is illegal in the UAE, and consequences can be severe. Celebrate responsibly and avoid any risky behavior.

Bahrain: Feeling the need for speed? Keep your racing ambitions off the public roads. Street racing is strictly prohibited in Bahrain, and hefty fines await those who break the law.

Kuwait: Need a power nap during your workday? Don't sleep on the job! Taking a nap at your workplace is frowned upon in Kuwait, so consider alternative ways to recharge during your lunch break.

36 - KANGAROO COURT: A LEGAL SAFARI OF STRANGENESS

Kangaroo Court: A Legal Safari of Strangeness

Ah, the Kangaroo Court, where justice sometimes hops around like a confused marsupial. These unofficial tribunals are less about logic and more about settling scores or settling stomachs (if someone ate the last meat pie, that is). So, put on your safari hats, folks, we're going on a tour of the weirdest, wildest, and frankly, wackiest court systems out there.

The Origin Story: Brace yourselves for a yarn wilder than a croc on the rampage. The "Kangaroo Court" nickname supposedly sprouted in Australia during the gold rush. Miners, facing disputes over nuggets and nuggets of wisdom (mostly about avoiding rogue emus), resorted to improvised courts led by whoever had the loudest voice and, often, the biggest beard. These kangaroo councils dispensed "justice" as quickly as you can say "bonzer," with verdicts ranging from "Oi, you nicked my shovel, hand it over!" to "Right-o, mate, settle this with a fisticuffs, winner takes all!"

Worst Legal Systems: A Hilarious (and Slightly Scary)

- North Korea: Where justice takes a vacation to the Gulag. Imagine a court system run by Kim Jong-un's hair stylist, and you're halfway there. Expect bizarre trials, questionable evidence like telepathic confessions, and sentences measured in years, not months.

- Florida: The Sunshine State, where legal weirdness thrives like mutant gators in the Everglades. From lawsuits over psychic attacks to the annual Squirrel Chili Cook-Off that somehow qualifies as legal evidence, Florida is a law library written by a tipsy flamingo.

- Louisiana: Where voodoo meets jurisprudence in a swampy legal gumbo. Gris-gris (magical charms) are considered admissible evidence, and judges might consult fortune tellers before issuing a verdict. Just don't ask why the courthouse smells like crawfish and incense.

- Thailand: Land of smiles, but don't step on the wrong one. Laws are about as flexible as a rubber band, and traffic regulations are basically suggestions made by friendly elephants. Just remember, jaywalking here might earn you a stern lecture from a monk and a puzzled look from a water buffalo.

- The Vatican City: Holy moly, the Pope has his own court system! Imagine tiny Swiss Guards in feathered hats handing out speeding tickets for chariot races and dealing with parking disputes involving angels. Divine intervention is probably par for the course here.

Remember, folks, while these legal systems might seem comical from afar, they can have serious consequences. Always research local laws before venturing into the legal wilderness, and if you find yourself in a Kangaroo Court, just play it cool, offer a friendly "G'day, mate," and hope your case doesn't get kangabbreviated.

THANK YOU

It's been a blast exploring the wacky world of laws and customs with you! I hope you found something informative, thought-provoking, and maybe even a little chuckle-worthy along the way.

Just a friendly reminder that some names and details might have been changed out of respect for legal restrictions in certain places. We strive to offer the most accurate information possible, but it's always wise to cross-check and do your own research before embarking on any real-life adventures, especially in sensitive regions.

So, as you go forth and explore the world, remember to pack your curiosity, your sense of humor, and a healthy dose of cultural sensitivity. And hey, if you stumble upon any quirky laws or hilarious customs, be sure to share them my way! I'm always up for a good story.

Until next time, happy travels and stay safe!

BNW

PUBLISH

Join us on your favourite platform, Scan the QR code on your phone or tablet

Thank you

Please review
on Amazon

B N William

Printed in Great Britain
by Amazon

42923465R00056